MW00757930

FIT MIND

+

FIT BODY

=

FIT LIFE

Because You Deserve This!

Trevor Buccieri

First published 2019 by 831 Designs London. UK
www.831designs.com
Book Creators and Publishers.

Copyright © 2019 by Trevor Buccieri.
All rights reserved.

No part of these pages, either text or image may be used
for any purpose other than personal use. Therefore,
reproduction, modification, storage in a retrieval system
or retransmission, in any form or by any means,
electronic, mechanical or otherwise, for reasons other than
personal use, is strictly prohibited without prior written
permission.

Book: Fit Mind + Fit Body = Fit Life
. Trevor Buccieri. -- 1st ed.

ISBN-: 9781797049823

DEDICATION

I dedicate this book to my family. To my mom and dad who have always believed in me and who have taught me how to be a man. To "the prettiest girl this side of Sandusky" my amazing wife Laura who completes me. To my three incredible sons Gavin, Grayson, and Roman who inspire me daily. And also to you, my extended family; words can't express my gratitude for your support, your application of this material and for having me be a part of your life. I love you all.

CONTENTS

INTRO

I never fully understood how profound of an impact the formula "fit mind plus fit body equals fit life" was having on my life and for all of us really. It's very simple. If you have a fit mind, you love yourself enough to understand what is most important to you and how your actions and inactions directly impact these things. A fit body is a body thriving through consistent nutrition and challenging workouts, enabling it to function at maximum capacity down to a cellular level. When you combine a fit mind with a fit body, this naturally accelerates and propels all other areas of your life, giving you a fit life, which is the life we all deserve.

Two years ago, I was involved in an ATV accident that immediately changed my life as I knew it. I completely destroyed my left wrist, had full reconstructive surgery, and found myself in a downward spiral of complacency, and just a plain old pile of shit filled with excuses and doubt. Little did I know this was the perfect environment for an upward explosion.

For the next year and a half, I completely shifted my actions and how I was spending my time. I was barely moving and certainly was not exercising. Because of this, my fit body dwindled over time and all but disappeared. My confidence was cut severely, but what was most challenging for me was that I felt I had lost my identity. It was a real pity party to say the least.

This was the first time I had taken an extended period of time away from exercise since I started my journey at 16 years old. I knew that a fit body was adding value to my life. What I didn't understand was how essential it is to keep a fit body during your most challenging times. This is your secret weapon preparing you for battle in all scenarios.

For several years previous, I had been studying and developing my fit mind, which I had during this entire experience. The problem was the lack I felt due to my missing fit body. This combination most certainly was not delivering the fit life I once knew, and the fit life I missed dearly. In fact, all areas of my life were being dragged through the dirt because of the fact that I had been dragging my fit body through the dirt.

For a year and a half, as my fit body broke down, I had rejected all the signs and messages my heart was telling me. Almost daily, there was a next-level solution waving over me and I ignored it. Because of this, I was blinded by what was happening right in front of my face. Over time, I began drifting with my nutrition, becoming more lenient because it was just all or nothing for me apparently. That isn't how it works and I knew this.

I had become the unfit fitness pro. I wasn't heavy. In fact, I was a skinny weakling. I weighed less than I did in high school and was at 19% body fat. Not what I call healthy. The biggest challenge however was that my perception and respect for myself had changed. This was affecting everything in my life, including my relationships, my ability to believe in myself, and my ability to fulfill my vision.

The beautiful lesson I learned here is that it's about resiliency and our ability to adapt quickly emotionally and physically to whatever we are handed.

At the time, I wasn't able to see how my actions and lack of actions were producing massive drawbacks to what is most important to me.

Looking back, this is the most challenging aspect of this experience for me. This is what I do and I had convinced myself I was all good when I knew inside I was far from good. Why did I ignore it? I know now. It's because I feared it. I was so deep inside the rabbit hole, I was uncertain of the way out and that stunted any action. It was time to make the choice and dig myself out.

Now that I have gone through this experience and again am living on the other side, I have a newfound understanding of, appreciation for and certainty in the fit body being the principal necessity for human performance and growth, rather than just an option or add-on. I'm truly grateful for my experience. Next time, there will not be a next time. I will not sacrifice this in my life again regardless of the circumstances.

Keeping my body in peak condition is a must, and I am now more certain than ever that it enables me to excel in everything I do further and beyond where I would be able to reach without it.

Although I wasn't functioning at maximum capacity when I decided to write this book, I was on the way up and was carrying a ton of responsibility on my shoulders. Now, I am 90% at my ultimate goal and I carry even more with a smile. The difference between me and many others is that many people complain about how much they have going on. I embrace it because I realize that, just like everyone else, I choose it. No person has to do anything. We choose what we do because it serves what is most valuable in our lives, period.

I hear people all the time complaining about their circumstances and all the stress that has forced its way into their lives. Let me make it very easy for you. You choose what you do and do not do. If you don't want to do something, then just don't do it. Complaining is not helping you or the others you surround yourself with. Resenting is preventing your ability to maximize your capacity. If you commit to it, crush it, otherwise, don't do it. That's it.

With many around me giving their opinions that I was so busy and that I should hold off on my book, as I listened to my gut, I realized that I needed to start the book one week ago. I knew this was exactly what would bring even more fulfillment into my life, so here we are.

While I was reading a book by Grant Cardone called *The 10x Rule*, there was a section that resonated big time with me. He said, "We need to honor who we are, and what we are and understand nobody can tell us what best to do for ourselves." We all make suggestions to our friends and loved ones based on our own values and observations only. We don't know the true internal wants and desires of others. Only an individual's heart knows this for certain and it needs to be heard.

Although this may seem obvious to you, it was more than a piece of information to me. It was a piece of information that connected the dots between several fields over many years. The takeaway was the simplicity of listening to how you feel in your heart, and acting on it. Don't overthink it. Surrender to it. So, I felt what was in my heart, listened to it and I went for it.

It's said that the way to fulfillment is simply following your heart. Now that I'm following, I'm writing this book and it lights me on fire because I know with every word I write, it creates greater opportunity for me to reach more people and serve them better.

Later in this book, I'll be introducing you to one of my mentors, Dr. John Demartini, whose teachings and influence have helped transform my life; to prepare you to crush and benefit from this book as designed, I strongly recommend going to www.drdemartini.com right now and completing the FREE Values Determination process before going any further. When you get to the page, see the menu on the left and click *"Determine Your Values."* This process will not only open your eyes to what you love most in your life, it will lay the foundation for you to explode your results from this book. Like I always say, if you are failing to prepare, you are preparing to fail.

THE TURNING POINT

This book is the product of the ideas I've had mingling in my head for some time. The reason I'm writing it now is because of this journey beginning with my ATV accident on August 9th 2015, which took a massive turn in January of 2017. The experience has been so significant and amazing to me that it became 100% necessary to put it on paper right now.

I can honestly say that the accident I was involved in two years ago has turned out to be one of the greatest, if not the greatest, transformation points I've had in my life to date.

Now, I will say, after the accident, it took some time for me to see it this way. Two minutes. That's right, two minutes. It took me two minutes to break through with gratitude and appreciation for the accident after it happened. This was the initial boundary I broke with my transformation.

This was the moment I realized all the countless hours of study and application were paying off. My life had been completely flipped upside down and I mentally adjusted to the circumstances in two minutes flat. I was equipped with a fit mind. I knew what was most important to me and I was able to see the new blessings in my life with what I would have previously strictly labeled a 'curse'.

However, my fit mind was immature because on the other side of the coin, I wasn't experienced enough to see that, over time, as I stopped working out and my body fell apart, so did all the other areas of my life. My recent transformation has thrown this realization into my life literally every single day since I recommitted myself to my fit body.

For the first several months after the accident, I was fine. In fact, I was really enjoying the fact that I was not able to work out and I had more time to spread to other things in my life. As more time passed, I knew I was a bit off, but the process of decline was so gradual I couldn't put a finger on what was going on. And even if I had, I would never have been able to accurately pinpoint the value I was missing out on in my life. I realized that, although I had not been working out, which takes time, I was actually losing time in my day. I began needing more sleep. I became less alert, less driven, less committed to and less confident in everything I was doing. I was sinking if not already sunk.

I think I had convinced myself that nutrition was still taking it home for me and I was all good. I excused myself from action with the famous response, "I CAN'T BECAUSE OF MY BROKEN BONES." Yes, of course, I could have. Let's face it... I just didn't. I was giving every excuse in the book and I was defeating myself. I'm so grateful the cards landed this way because the impact when I did start back up was literally so abrupt and instant in all areas of my life that I couldn't ignore it. I had to start documenting my life transformation on paper and deliver the magic formula to as many hands as possible because of the massive value I know it will add to all lives.

January of 2017 marks the time when I made the choice to get back my fit body. From the moment that choice was made, all areas of my life began shifting and have been accelerating ever since.

I transformed my body and got "it" back in just under four months. What has changed for me in the last four months in my eyes is unbelievable at worst. All other areas of my life have exploded massively. I have a fit mind, which I've conditioned for years, so I have defined what is most important to me and understand how my actions impact these same things. That said, for quite some period of time, I neglected the physical fit body, which slowed my progress down considerably in all other areas of my life. The scary part is that I didn't even see it. Simply put, I had a fit mind without a fit body, leaving me with a semi-fit life, not a maximized fit life. As soon as I began transforming my body again, my life went into hyper acceleration mode in all areas. At that moment, it became 100% apparent to me what had been missing and also that I had been blind to the fact until I brought it back into my life.

We've all heard the saying, "I didn't know what I had until it was gone." True. What also holds true is that when we lose something gradually over time, as opposed to abruptly, it's different. It becomes harder to notice and identify because our bodies are built to survive in all conditions and we adjust to our environment. So I'd like to add, "I didn't know what was missing in my life until I had it again."

My experience has enabled me to confirm with certainty the power of this and I have since conditioned my mind even further to better understand and analyze the effects transforming our bodies has on all other areas of our lives. It was so organic and apparent to me that I needed to share it with you.

The closer I've moved towards my fit body goal throughout this experience, the faster and more significant the transformation and presence of opportunities have been appearing in all areas of my life. Seeing this has built the value in keeping my fit body at all costs. It simply is not an option any longer ever again. It has now become a MUST.

The biggest takeaway I've learned from this experience is that it all begins and ends with our own self-perception. When we love ourselves for exactly who we are and where we are in our growth and development as a person, we exude this in all we do and every person we surround ourselves with feels it. On the other hand, when we don't love ourselves for exactly who we are and where we are in our growth and development as a person, we show it and every person we surround ourselves with also feels this.

Let me ask you a question... Do you like to surround yourself with people who lift you up and make you stretch yourself or do you like to surround yourself with those who drag you down? Pretty obvious question I know. The reason I ask this is to give us all a moment to reflect on the energy we are bringing into others' lives. Are we bringing energy of lack, excuses and complacency? If so, what value are we adding to others around us? Now flip the paper over and imagine the value you would be giving others and receiving in return by showing up and giving off energy of abundance, solutions and endless possibilities. Quite a difference. This is exactly what has happened for me.

I use nutrition and exercise as tools to create a fit body, giving me an accelerative, progressive, thriving environment for my soul to live in and use to fulfill my dreams. It's my temple just as your body is yours.

If you want to go to the next level in your life, why not equip yourself with a fit body and explode your progress?

Maybe you say you don't have a fit body and you already are successful in business or whatever area of life you hold dear to you. Honestly, I'm thrilled for you for real. At the same time,

I'm concerned for you. There needs to be attention brought to the fact that if your body is not fit, you are short-changing yourself. You are failing to maximize your true capacity in areas you may be lacking and especially in areas you hold dearest that you may feel you are dominating right now. Most importantly, you deserve this. You deserve everything you dream of and you deserve to get there as fast as possible.

I'll tell you what. Commit to a fit body for just six short weeks. I'm certain the experience will be magical and completely transformative for you.

Just six months ago, I was in a hole in all areas of my life compared to where I was before my accident and I was oblivious to what was really going on. Looking back, I can now see that the key is that I had lost respect for myself, which affected everything.

As I started going through this process of self-discovery and "rebirth", I quickly realized I was not alone. People all around me were also transforming their bodies, were drastically transforming in all other areas of their lives just as I had been. What I have found with many of these same people is that the severity of the transformation hasn't been fully understood and recognized. If we aren't able to understand and recognize something, we aren't able to grasp the full value it is adding to our lives and it becomes very easy to allow ourselves to slip backwards to where we once came from.

Throughout this book, you will hear my complete story and the stories of several people just like you who are crushing it and maximizing all areas of their lives because they have a fit mind plus a fit body.

"Faith is taking the first step even when you don't see the whole staircase."

Martin Luther King, Jr.

FROM BOY TO SCHOLAR

My name is Trevor Buccieri and I'm a life transformation specialist ... although it wasn't always this way.

I grew up battling my weight along with constant habits of binge eating. I'll delve into more about that later, but this eventually led me into my own personal weight loss journey and transformed my body. What was most interesting was the fact that my body was not the only area of my life that was transformed—everything had changed for me. Everything had gone next level and I didn't understand it, but man I remember it like yesterday because it excited me to the point where, for the first time in my life, I felt as though I caught a glimpse of my calling.

I wanted to know "Is this just me or is this a reoccurring constant? Does transforming your body naturally perpetuate and accelerate transformation in all other areas of life?" I made it my mission right then and there to put this puzzle together, package it into a solution and share it with the world. I didn't know it, but what I was searching for at the time is what I call the fit mind.

I began savagely devouring everything I could get my hands on about nutrition, exercise and human behavior. This led me to becoming one of the top weight loss and body transformation experts in the industry. This entire experience lit me up and still does to this day. Having the opportunity to learn how to transform the body and, most importantly, gaining a sense of command and certainty with my methods has been completely empowering.

For several years following, I spent thousands upon thousands of hours applying, studying, and collaborating with many of the greats around the world to become a master of my craft and create my own personal transformation formula I would soon deliver to the masses. It was time to give back to others the gifts I had been blessed with in my own life.

The foundational principle I've adopted as a model of the way I choose to live my life is reciprocity. Reciprocity is "an exchange of opportunity given to you and then passed on to others." I feel so blessed to have found something I love but also something that has completely changed my life. Now it's incredible to me that I have the opportunity to take everything I've learned and applied in my own life and deliver profound results to others in a simple package. I'm truly grateful.

As I opened my first brick-and-mortar establishment, it soon became very obvious that if I were going to live my mission of taking the solution I had in my hands and share it with the world, I had to do much more than I was doing. Mastering the body transformation product in terms of exercise and nutrition, although crucial, was not the only thing I needed for this to be a success. I needed to learn how to scale what I was doing faster and more effectively while, at the same time, learning to manage the growth. Soon after opening my first location, it was even more apparent that, if I was going to make my vision a reality, I needed to understand business. And just knowing about business wasn't going to be enough. Mastering business and applying everything I learned with massive action became another MUST.

This began my lifelong intensive dive into education, where I've committed to exposing myself to as many fields of study and personal development as I'm able to swallow. Principles of success in life, business success, business development, human behavior, time management, team management, personal management, marketing, leadership, team-building, creating culture, creating experiences, sales, sales and more sales, statistical analysis, accounting, emotional intelligence, communication and relationship-building, body language, team management, innovation and ideation, team recruiting, technology education, metrics, statistics, quantification, key performance indicators, business success principles, marketing, branding, public speaking, music, systemization, scaling ideas, scaling businesses and the list continues to grow as I study more today than I ever have in my life. It inspires me, it lights my passion on fire, and it fulfills me more each day because I can feel the continuous transformation in my life, and I know I am moving towards making my vision a reality.

It's very interesting when you look at human behavior. We are very predictable and emotional beings. Every action of what we do or do not do is an expression of how we feel at the time, nothing less and nothing more. Education and intelligence were always something I felt disempowerment and lack about, wearing it throughout my life in the form of self-doubt. Feeding that daily with more and more knowledge fills this void for me. So much so that, year after year, I have committed to increasing my studies.

Continually studying, learning and improving have transformed the mental area of my life and have ultimately changed my perception of my abilities and the value of what I have to give. I now see myself as I've always desired to: I am a leader. I also realize what it has taken to build this self-perception and that continual accelerated growth is necessary for me to keep growing.

A mentor of mine, Pat Rigsby, said, "Every day, you are either getting better or you are getting worse. There is no in between." So either you are taking action to ensure you are growing or you are not. I choose action each and every day. I adopted that principle into my life years ago because I understood the value it was delivering in all areas of my life. It's become a habit for me.

At this point in my life, I refuse to be anything less than the best because I know I am capable. Diversified education has become the gateway for me. I realized that in order to be taken seriously with what I was out to achieve, I needed to take myself seriously by preparing, which meant a whole lot of education. Becoming a trailblazer on the cutting edge of body and life transformations along with business mastery and business transformation coaching became the necessary step one in my journey towards impacting millions.

I became intrigued and obsessed with all of the intricacies of business as I realized this was on the way for me rather than in the way. Mastering it became an inspired game for me. Quickly learning to run towards failure in my business enabled me to transform and rebrand my own business as it evolved from an idea into a national brand.

Opening my brick-and-mortar locations, now under the brand Core Capacity Transformations™, has been one of the most enjoyable and fulfilling opportunities I've ever had. It's created a platform to take everything I've learned and applied in my own life and deliver profound results to people everywhere in a simple package. This same system has now transformed thousands of lives and continues transforming more every single day. That means the world to me and pushes me harder. I'm grateful.

As I continued exploding my own business and knowledge base, I found myself receiving multiple referrals of new business transformation coaching clients and began being approached by many entrepreneurs wanting to coach under my business transformation program. This was incredible to me because it was exactly what I wanted to be doing and it was happening at full speed.

This massive growth has led me to collaborate with an entirely new network of amazing mentors and colleagues who have not only become great friends, but some of them have also become business transformation coaching clients of mine.

Coaching other entrepreneurs has become therapeutic in a way to me. Not only do I love being able to help people transform and become empowered through their businesses, it has also become a secret weapon of mine. Every day, I get to visit different areas of business as I coach others, causing me to reflect, re-innovate and continually take massive action towards mastery.

Now, we have all heard the phrase "knowledge is power." I disagree. Knowledge and know-how are extremely important, but without action they mean nothing. Knowledge we have gained is nothing more than potential power until it is set into motion through taking massive action. Knowing and practicing this consistently is called wisdom.

Overall, my journey has been anything but rainbows and butterflies and for that I'm also grateful. I've been handed as well as created many roadblocks and extreme challenges along the way, which have led me to stretch myself to find the answers to questions I never would have had to ask and seek out had I not taken this course of action.

"Understand that it is ok to be scared or uncertain, however right beyond those barriers ultimately lie your dreams."

Josh Hinds

MY TRANSFORMATION: QUICK TAKEAWAYS

Through my ATV accident two years ago, I was given the unique experience as a transformation specialist to completely regress from peak physical conditioning all the way back to square one. It has been the most incredible experience being able to start from nothing and completely rebuild myself.

Remastering the fit body has transformed my life in ways I would have told you were impossible if I weren't living it myself.

Simply looking at how I view myself has changed everything. I am back in line with my spiritual mission and my confidence and self-awareness have exploded. I'm more financially organized and prepared. I am more fulfilled as a leader and provider for my family. My business is exploding with beeline focus on massive impact and contribution on a global scale. I am meeting more people I can serve and collaborate with on a daily basis.

I attribute the root of this being the conditioning of my fit body enabling all of this to drive to the max. I know that if I were only in half the condition I am in now, I wouldn't be close to where everything is in my life at this point.

At the same time, there was something else driving me to start fast and finish strong every day with this mission of achieving my fit body that I hadn't fully grasped the power of. There was struggle, there was challenge, and there was pain that may have previously led me to give up and quit, but I didn't because I had a fit mind and it has pulled me through. All along, I knew I deserved better and now that I am deep into my fit body transformation, having a fit mind enables me to clearly see the value that achieving a fit body has added to all areas of my life. I have been able to literally watch my life transform in all areas throughout this experience.

It was empowering because it was so distinct and concrete that it's given me certainty in what I have experienced. It wasn't about fearing the struggle and it wasn't even about the goal itself. It was about what was going to be enabled in my life once I achieved my fit body goal. This knowledge gave me clear understanding and appreciation for the value and true-life impact attaining a fit body has. Knowing this gave me staying power through the struggles because of the big-picture value I was in hot pursuit of gaining, and now keeping, in my life.

Looking back, I know I never would have been able to go at it as aggressively and focused as I did had I not first built my fit mind. Having a fit mind helped me understand the big picture. The big picture was the vision of what I wanted my life to be and the realization and understanding that my fit body transformation was going to enable me to get it.

Realizing this as I began my transformation gave me fuel along the way during challenging times and kept me focused. It's also built insane value in keeping myself at my peak, realizing that when I let it go, everything in my life also drops off in parallel. Why? It comes down to the simple fact that when my cells aren't firing to the max, I begin to view myself differently, I carry myself with less certainty and send off a lower energy to those around me, all leading to myself and others perceiving me as less capable as a leader.

Do I care what others think of me? No, because I know everything I do comes directly from my heart and comes from love, but I will also answer yes to the same question. My mission and purpose are to be a leader in my field and serve others. If I am not holding myself at the highest level, which is deserved by those I'm serving and quite frankly required by the best leaders, then yes, I care with 200% of my soul. If that is the case, I am not fulfilling my personal mission here on Earth, which is to transform lives with inspired solutions.

"The true test of a man's character is what he does when no one is watching."

John Wooden

WHY FIT MIND + FIT BODY = FIT LIFE

Through my experience, I believe that transforming the physical area of your life is the greatest catalyst to transforming all areas of life, giving you a fit life.

So you may be wondering why fit mind + fit body = fit life and why not just a fit body = fit life. The fit mind needs to be established first and foremost to gain an understanding of the true impact of any goal. As people, we never do anything in our lives unless we benefit from it. If we haven't wrapped our mind around the benefits attaining and maintaining a fit body will have in our lives, how will we get through the challenges that go along with getting and keeping the fit body? In this case, we haven't created enough value and it becomes easier to just walk away and give up.

Taking the time to earn a fit mind is the greatest expression of loving yourself because it means you truly want to understand how you operate. It means you have specifically identified what is most important to you in your life and can see how your choices and actions directly impact those same things.

If we don't understand how what we do and do not do affects everything, it's impossible for us to identify and visualize the results we want.

Life is not happening to us but created by us through choice and response. We create our entire life through choosing the actions we take and the actions we don't take.

Through having a fit mind, I have continued to see the power of the fit body and what it has added and continues to add in my life. That said, why has the process become easier to commit to over the years when everything would tell me the discipline would grow more boring, repetitive and tedious over time?

Only one thing could be powerful enough to lead to this result and it is choice—a choice to take action because I've done the work of identifying with my fit mind what I get in return for achieving a fit body. I admit it's a choice I've grown more committed to over time as I continue seeing the transformations in all areas of my life flourishing.

My fit mind understands the value transforming my body adds to what is most important to me in my life and it immediately goes from, *I should transform my body because my doctor says to* or *because the BMI chart says I'm overweight*, to *I MUST transform my body because of the life I want and the life I know it will help enable.*

Every great accomplishment we have begins with a shift in our mind where we make a choice to make something happen no matter what challenge gets in our way. Regardless of the circumstances of pain or pleasure, you have reached the point where it has become a must in your life if you are willing to endure both sides to attain it. Many of us have goals and yet many of them are stagnant with zero progress, sometimes infinitely. Just like it is said, when the pain of staying the same is greater than the pain of change, change happens.

What I have seen through my life and observed in so many others is that we haven't learned and applied a method to build enough value to our own lives to make it a must. When we learn this process, we achieve what I call a fit mind. We are able to see how taking massive action towards our goals through choice has the power to completely transform our lives. Why would we want to do this? Because we deserve it.

Let me ask you a question, who is responsible for you? That's right, you and only you.

If you said someone else, I'm here to say I love you and it's time to wake up because your thoughts are misguided. Even if you are still living under your parents' roof and you are 14 years old or whatever the case, you are still in charge of your own choices regardless of how you slice it.

So now let's talk about the greatest and most under-maximized tool we all have at our disposal, the weapon capable of turning our greatest dreams into reality—the fit body.

Our body is our vessel. It is our home. If we don't take care of our body, how can we best serve ourselves and others? The answer quite simply is that we cannot. If your home has shingles falling off, holes in the walls and broken windows, is it best prepared to weather the storm and fulfill its purpose? Wouldn't you want to fix it? Our body is no different. If it is not properly prepared and harnessed, it's physiologically impossible for us to maximize our capacity on this earth.

Through my own personal journey to the fit body along with coaching thousands of others through their transformations, it's become very clear that transforming the physical area of our lives leads to transformation in all other areas of our lives.

Utilizing the principles of the fit mind, you are able to ask and answer the question, "How will your fit body transformation benefit what is most important to you in your life?" Taking the time to thoroughly answer such a simple question will enable you to clearly see the true value attaining and keeping the fit body will deliver to all areas of your life.

Mastering the fit body is going to accelerate the accomplishment of your goals in all other areas of your life simply because you are strengthening the functionality of your body down to a cellular level.

Working backwards, to achieve a fit life, we maximize every cell in our body by physically transforming and achieving a fit body. To achieve and maintain our fit body, we must understand the value a fit body adds to our lives by first understanding and attaining the fit mind.

Fit mind plus fit body equals fit life. Breaking the chain by excluding the mind or body from the equation creates a sub-par incomplete fit life formula with sub-par results, period.

"The whole is greater than the sum of its parts."

Aristotle

MY STORY: PART 1

Almost daily I have the opportunity to share my story with others who find it hard to believe my past is the story about a boy growing up overweight and disempowered.

Up until I was eight years old, I was about as active as they come. I was all over the neighborhood on my bike, involved in all types of sports and still I had plenty of energy to harass my younger brother Tyler.

When I was eight, things were put on hold a bit as I ran into a kidney problem. Long story short and three surgeries in one summer later, I was in recovery and on the up and up. However, my activities were put to an abrupt halt at the same time. Doctor's orders, I was to remain as sedentary as possible until further notice. To an overly active eight-year-old kid, this was pretty far out of my comfort zone.

I needed something else I could spend my time and energy enjoying. I soon established a very tight-knit relationship with Hostess snack cakes, Little Debbie everything, and radio-controlled cars.

My days consisted of eating, sitting and steering my cars for quite a while, as I remember. Apparently, I had taken the doctor's suggestions a bit further than prescribed. In fact, looking back, I see now that I took this experience as the opportunity to dig myself into the deepest hole I could imagine. For this, I am eternally grateful because the same hole is where I found my purpose.

Growing up overweight gave me the gift of understanding why I am who I am and why I do what I do without judgment for myself. It gave me the gift of empathy for others going through something I can 100% relate to. I've been there; I've climbed, I've fallen, gotten back up again and become stronger, just as I'm certain others can do.

The summer before my senior year, my good friend Todd Zandrowicz approached me and said, "Man, you should play football." I thought, *Why the hell not?* and committed to it. As soon as I did, Todd quickly brought me into the weight room and began introducing me to my future.

Two weeks into training, things were changing not only on the outside but actually more so on the inside. I began walking differently. I began having conversations with people I would never have had the courage to speak with before.

I remember thinking to myself, *Do people know about this shit?* It was like I had found the Holy Grail or the fountain of transformation. It was like magic, so simple and yet so complex at the same time. But just like anything, by taking simple steps over and again consistently over a long period of time, you become a master. Just like any other challenge worth committing to in our lives.

As I continued my pursuit of my fit body into my college years, I found myself naturally progressing into a coach as I began working with many students and the faculty with their own transformations. I remember several times during these experiences getting a vision of helping millions of people transform their bodies and their lives. People just like me who feel that the way they look, feel and put themselves out there is holding them back from maximizing their capacity in life. It was at that point I realized the extreme impact achieving my fit body was having on all areas of my life. Sharing this with others became my focus and obsession.

Although I have no idea how, just following this has led me here. When the goal is clear and the why is strong enough, the hows take care of themselves. My own personal transformation has been a 22-year journey of ups and downs as I learned to better gain control over my perceptions and sob stories.

Two years ago, I was at a place where I was pleased with myself. I was happy. I had been through it all, found what worked best for me, and maximized my fit mind and my fit body.

But as they say, what goes up must come down.

August 9th, 2015 marks a date I will always remember. This was the day I was handed an extreme challenge I didn't know I was ready for. I was in a serious ATV accident leaving me with a severely broken left wrist needing surgery as well as a broken right hand. Oops.

Luckily, I had been training for this moment for years. Two minutes after the accident happened and I had gathered myself, I was able to see the immediate and massive benefits of the situation. I was broken and in a lot of pain, but I was good with it and ready to get started on the next chapter.

The universal law of polarity says there are two sides to every situation. The difference between the two extremes of one thing is called polarity. They are on opposite ends of the spectrum, hence the saying "polar opposite." There is light and there is dark. There is an up and there is a down. There is hot and there is cold. These, in fact, are the same thing. Both hot and cold are temperatures, only they are located on opposite ends of the pole. To drive the point further, the law of synchronicity says that both sides actually occur simultaneously. So while we may perceive something is hot, it is also cold relative to the heat of the sun, for example. It's all in the eyes of the person perceiving it relative to the context of the situation.

Knowing and practicing these principles is what got me through the mess. One of my great mentors, Dr. John Demartini, said, "The quality of your life is based on the quality of the questions you ask."

When I was on the ground and had realized what had happened, I decided to ask myself a quality question. "How does this accident benefit what is most important to me in my life?"

Answering this was revealing and completely inspiring. My focus and values immediately changed as I put the pieces of the puzzle together. I could no longer work out, so I decided I would put extra time into studying nutrition, spending time with my family, which was lacking, and remastering my vision and mission of extending my reach to serve millions of people losing millions of pounds.

In the beginning, things were great! I was really enjoying the time I had gained back from not working out. I was on point with everything I was now focusing on. My nutrition was at a whole new level with what I was learning and applying. Months had gone by and I still looked like I was in shape even though now I know I was only fooling myself.

Use it or lose it. This holds true in everything I have ever come across and this is what began happening to my fit body over time. I wasn't using it, and I slowly began losing it until it was gone. It's scary because the process was so gradual that I wasn't even able to detect it until I found myself sitting there one day saying, "What the hell happened to me?" My fit body was gone and my confidence had dwindled along with it.

It had been 1.5 years to the day since I had done my last workout. Bottom line, I fed myself excuses saying, *As soon as I heal, I'll be back at it.* I set myself up for failure and did the same thing I have been coaching people not to do for years. Long story short, it never fully healed and over the course of those 1.5 years, my body fell apart. I'm grateful for this lesson hitting so deep. What I ultimately learned is that the time was, is and always will be now. Do it now. No time will ever be the perfect time, but the perfect time to move forward is now.

The first days back at the gym were extremely humbling. Either way, I was over it and committed to the ride. To be honest, it was more than just the first few days that were humbling. It was more like the first several months back. Not only was I reteaching my body from ground zero, but also I was quickly learning the limitations I had due to my recent injuries. Then the day came when I had the workout where I surprised myself. Game over. I was back in the groove.

As I continued training hard into month three, my fit body was making a strong comeback. Not only that, but everything in my life was moving at a completely new tempo. I was aware of the changes that were happening around me because I was much more invested in the growth than simply being along for the ride. That said, I hadn't taken the time to fully reflect on the direct correlation between my fit body transformation and the transformations happening in all other areas of my life. The further I was getting towards my goal, the more all other areas of my life were taking off.

When I did take a look, it was mind-blowing, undeniable and also very abrupt. Spiritually, I felt on track with my mission. Mentally, my confidence and perception of myself literally turned back on. Financially, I began putting into action a stronger plan to contribute more to a greater number of people by bringing my business to the next level. With my family, I began to show up more. I have been much more present with my family. Vocationally, my business growth has exploded into next gear, which is inspiring because our impact reach is expanding daily and I feel it. We are now focused on opening multiple locations throughout the US and also internationally. Socially, I've been able to put a better version of myself out there, which has opened up numerous new opportunities already. Physically, I'm getting closer to my ultimate goal each and every day.

I've even noticed differences in the way I am leading on an everyday basis. I've become more truthful to everyone I come across, truthful in a sense that I am much more direct than I have been in the past. I feel we all have a tendency to sugar-coat feedback we give to others through fear of hurting their feelings. I have lived in this box for far too long. Looking back, the most profound growth experience I've ever had was when one of my mentors told it to me exactly how it is. I know now that failing to give this to others is a disservice to them. What they do with the information once they have it is then up to them.

My decision-making has become much quicker and filled with certainty. I've become much more forward thinking while at the same time staying focused on the now.

I feel free and the best part is that I'm not alone here. Others are exploding their life transformations all around by us utilizing the same principles I'm laying out for you here. I can't wait to share some of their stories with you later in the book.

Having been through multiple ups and downs in my own body transformation journey, what I do know is that the body is very resilient. It is built to survive in any way it can and it is easily able to transition and adjust to so many circumstances of non-optimal conditions. As my fit body declined and hit rock bottom, yes, I can say I was surviving, but I most certainly was not thriving.

Now that I have a better understanding of just how resilient the body actually is, I can see just how difficult it is to identify the exact point where we peak and then begin to regress with our fit bodies.

The great news is that it's all based on behaviors. Things we decide to do or not do. This means it is possible to identify this point if we are willing to track our behaviors and emotions daily and quantify them regularly. This will enable you to see a direct correlation between the progress of your fit body and the actions you are taking to run towards it. Massive action will lead to massive progress towards your fit body. Less than massive action simply will not.

What I recommend is, if you are about to begin your own transformation, you begin tracking this material throughout the experience. This will help you during any stick points in your progress where you will be able to see a direct correlation between the actions you are taking and the results you are receiving due to these actions. Ninety-nine times out of 100, when results begin to plateau, it's directly because of the actions or lack of action we are taking.

It's been one hell of a journey so far and what I do know at this point is that the results myself and others have received is unbelievable at worst. It tells me that regardless of anything going on in my life, the continuation of feeding my body exactly what it wants and pushing it physically to advance will be a constant for me moving forward. It is my enabler.

Connecting the dots from the past 20 years of my research and due to recent events, it's become more and more clear that what people have been experiencing through their body transformations isn't just theory. It's 100% real down to a cellular level. Physical body transformation accelerates and enhances transformation in all areas of life.

Bruce Lipton, a world-renowned developmental biologist, said the cell is affected by everything we do and do not do. If we are dehydrated, all cells are dehydrated and compensating. If we are thriving, all cells are thriving. The foods we put in our bodies are crucial, and the conditioning of our bodies through challenging exercise enables us to best process and utilize these foods to our greatest advantage. Embracing and practicing this is the difference between every cell being in an acidic fight or flight, sympathetic nervous system environment and every cell being in an alkaline rested, prepared and focused parasympathetic nervous system environment. It is the difference between merely surviving and completely thriving.

The great Jim Rohn said, "Treat your body like a temple, not a woodshed." It's the greatest enabler in our lives. He said, "The mind and body work together making it crucial for the body to be a strong support system for the mind and spirit. If you take good care of it, your body can take you wherever you want to go, with the power, strength, energy and vitality you will need to get there." He also said that "many people don't do well because they don't feel well." I think that's beautifully put and it doesn't get any simpler than that. If your mind is strong but your body is weak to the point it's preventing you from fulfilling your life, and you want improvement, it's about time you take a good look at it, step up to the plate, own it and change it so it begins working for you instead of you working for it.

If you really want what you say you want in your life, you owe it to yourself to create a fit body support system to help propel and accomplish your ambitions and your dreams. It's your greatest asset and tool to create whatever you desire for your life, if only you show it the respect and care it deserves. Maximizing the capacity of every cell in your body enables your body to best serve you.

Just as in any relationship, communication is everything. Here we are talking about the communication you have with your body and it's very simple. On a scale of 1–10, how do I feel today? On a scale of 1–10, where is my energy level today? A very large contributor to how we answer these questions has to do with our nutrition and exercise regime.

For example, most practice nutrition with a mainstream approach. This is the hot information we find all over the internet, TV, tabloids, pop culture and advertisements. As we absorb this information and make our decisions based upon it, we approach our nutrition just like the golden rule of doing unto others. We begin feeding our bodies the foods we would want others to feed us to increase our fit body.

We hear things like organic, gluten-free, fat-free, carb-free, vegan, etc. and are led to believe that as long as we stay in these categories, we are good to go. Now, don't get me wrong. All of these things are great, but the context these are used in on the surface is fuzzy. In other words, there is organic, gluten-free, fat-free, carb-free, vegan garbage that will not actually help you at all. Let me ask you... Do you really think organic, gluten-free, fat-free, carb-free, vegan pizza is really going to help your body thrive or would fruit be better?

Do you feel if you had a clearer understanding of exactly what your body needs nutritionally in order to thrive, you would be capable of better results?

In comes the platinum rule of nutrition. The platinum rule says, "Treat others how they want to be treated." This takes relationship building to a whole new level because it requires us to take the time to learn about another's values and then treat them accordingly. The platinum rule of nutrition is no different. Feed your body what it actually wants to be fed and it will thrive for you. Our intention is to create a thriving body, capable of being an asset in our lives. The only way we can accomplish this is to learn about the intricacies of human nutrition and apply this learned information consistently with massive action. Only then will we gain a strong understanding of what the body truly wants.

Doing this, we will learn to eat how we want to feel. We will learn to listen to the feedback our bodies give us continuously, which many are not in tune with. This is why I have dedicated much of my life to mastering the study of nutrition as a whole. It intrigues me, and the further I dive into it, the more I find to learn about. My personal mission with nutrition is to continue studying the make-up of the body down to a cellular level, learning exactly what I need to completely thrive and feed myself only that. I feel there are many other barriers to break through here that we haven't even tapped into yet.

Everything has been exploding for me the last six months or so, and none of this was happening before I began remastering my body. I was progressing in my life but more at a snail's pace. My mind was there. I understood how my actions were impacting what I hold most dear and at that time I was happy with my development. What I was negligent of, however, was what I was missing out on. I wasn't using my turbo button, my secret weapon I had access to the entire time.

I had cancelled my fit body out of my life, which I hadn't done since I was 17 years old, and my progress slowed down. I know this now because since my recent personal body transformation, everything in my life is in explosion mode. The better my fit body becomes, the more my focus acceleration and progress increases three if not fivefold in all areas of my life.

I had simply crawled back into the same hole I had dug myself out of long ago and I didn't even realize it. Then I broke back out of my shell yet again. Now I will never go back. I see the repercussions like I never have before.

I'll say it again and again throughout this book because it bears repeating in order to fully devour it. The transformation of your body is the greatest catalyst for explosive transformation in all other areas of your life. Whatever your goals, I'm saying that transforming your body will get you there and beyond in hyper drive.

So what about you? Do you have goals? Would you like to explode your progress? What if I told you all you needed to do to make that happen is to define what is most important to you in your life and transform your body? Does that sound too good to be true? Would that be valuable if that were all there was to it?

Well, I challenge you to try it for yourself if you think you're worth it. I believe everyone deserves and owes it to themselves to maximize their capacity here on Earth and to be fulfilled. If transforming our bodies enables us to live our dreams more efficiently and more effectively, I'll be drinking that Kool-Aid all day long. I challenge you for 30 days to work out and follow a six meal per day plan; then, at the end, reflect on the transformation in all areas of your life. Later in this book, I'll give you an easy, done-for-you nutrition program and a very simple full body workout you can pick up right away and let your fit body transformation begin.

What will this do for you moving forward? Imagine how it feels when you are lost in any area of your life. Imagine feeling disconnected and disempowered in any way, shape or form. You may be there right now. Now imagine breaking the boundaries you've created for yourself and being freed of these chains. This is what it will do for you moving forward. The short answer to the question is that it will do everything.

The first 30 days of your challenge will pose as a sample of what is to come in the next 30 days, 60 days and beyond as you earn your fit body. The more you improve your fit body, the faster all areas of your life will continue to accelerate into new orbits. Continue after the 30-day mark and I guarantee at your next 30-day reflection point, you will see the steady accelerative growth in all areas of your life.

Now, of course, I want to be clear in saying that this all depends on whether you are actually challenging yourself daily with constantly improving your nutrition and exercise efforts, giving your body no choice but to transform. What I'm not talking about is just going through the motions and half-assing it. This will lead to exactly the same growth impact in all other areas of life. Improvements? Yes, but only half-assed improvements compared to what you deserve to achieve and are more than capable of.

I remember reaching a point where I was asking myself, "So which one leads to a fit life ... is it the fit mind or the fit body?" The answer was both. This led to another question. "Which one comes first in the process?" The answer was the fit mind. Because whatever the mind conceives and believes it can achieve. When the mind is decided and focused, the body simply follows. If the mind can't see how our actions will benefit what is most important to us in our lives, there isn't enough value in the end product for us to take action.

So if the fit mind is the first crucial step in attaining a fit life, then how do you get a fit mind, right? I've got great news for you. I'm going to show you exactly how and it starts by first beginning to track where you are right now.

Tracking Your Progress and Emotions Daily: Keep a daily journal tracking the following four metrics.

1. *Did my accumulative actions today help me get better and closer to my goals? _____ If no, explain.*

_____

2. *On a scale of 1–10, where am I emotionally today?*
   _____

3. *On a scale of 1–10, how do I feel today?* _____
4. *On a scale of 1–10, how is my energy today?* _____

THE FIT MIND

The fit mind is a mind conditioned to progressively master our emotions. The fit mind has identified what is most important to us in our lives, known as our highest values, and understands how everything we choose to do or not do affects these values directly. It's a mind aligned with what the heart is communicating with it. This creates a massive amount of value for us because it teaches us to listen to what we really want in our lives and to love ourselves enough to understand why.

The universal law of polarity says everything has two sides. Its upside and its downside. Its front and its backside. At the same time, it shows us that both the front and the back possess blessings. It exists to enable us to learn that inside of every failure is also success, and within every loss, there is victory. It exists in order for us to experience life to the fullest. It's all in how we choose to look at it. We could choose to look at a situation inside of a closed box, only experiencing a single-sided polarized viewpoint. We can also choose to look at both sides of the coin for everything the situation offers. When we embrace the entire picture, we learn how the same things that repel us also add a massive amount of value to our lives.

When we are blinded and can only focus on the downside of a situation, a fit mind asks how the same situation benefits what is most important to us in our lives, our highest values. Every single person has an individualized set of values, a prioritized list specific to each person of what is most important to them in their lives. Everything in life that occurs is considered an event. Every person labels the event differently according to their values. If we choose to see an event as good, it's because it supports our personal values. If we choose to see an event as bad, it's because it challenges our personal values. It's all in the eyes of who perceives it because it supports our personal values. If we choose to see an event as bad, it's because it challenges our personal values. It's all in the eyes of who perceives it.

The universal law of synchronicity brings this to the next level. This law states both sides of polarity occur simultaneously at all times. It's all a matter of our perspective. Where there is light, there is also dark. Where there is right, there is also wrong. Where there is good, there is also bad all at the same time. Asking ourselves the right questions is all that is needed to unlock the other side. If we only see the drawbacks, what are the benefits of the same situation to our highest values? If we only see the benefits, what are the drawbacks of the same situation to our highest values?

This brings me to a very common question: why would I want to ever look at the drawbacks of a situation when I only see good? I don't want to change how I feel.

When I began studying these laws, this was my initial thought process. If I were in bliss, why would I want to distract that by thinking about the drawbacks of the situation? For me, the best way I can describe it is that it centers me. It balances my emotions and, in turn, my actions. It enables me to not be blinded by the fantasy that life can only be one way or it is not perfect. I was missing half of the puzzle and arguably perhaps the most important half. I was missing my desire to see the challenges in my life, not recognizing that the challenges are the only things that deliver uncertainty and ultimately growth in our lives. I now desire and am able to see all situations for what they are. There are both benefits and drawbacks to all situations. Studying this continually has given me clarity and potential power. Applying it continually will bring me wisdom.

A fit mind is a mind that understands exactly why we are attracted to some things and repelled by others. It either adds value to what is most important to us, which we label as good, or it challenges what is most important to us, which we label as bad. What's most interesting in the equation of learning and acquiring a fit mind is the fact that the mind does not initiate our perceptions and gut feelings. The heart does.

The mind makes decisions, but the heart guides us. Science is now rekindling the past works of ancient philosophers and past religious teachings uncovering the proof that the heart is in fact the center of our soul or being.

Over the past 20 years, it's been proven that the heart is the first physiological respondent to all situations in our lives. The heart actually perceives an event and responds by initiating a change in heart rhythm. It then sends the signals associated with the change in rhythm to the brain through what is called cardio-electromagnetic communication. The brain receives the heart's signal, reads it, and what many refer to as "the gut feeling" is then produced.

It's interesting because what we know as "the gut feeling" is actually much more than that. Looking a bit deeper into it, we see there's much more beauty and grace to the process. The information we receive in the mind about an event is our intuition delivered via a direct message from our heart. The heart picks up signals around an event, interprets them compared to how they directly impact our highest values, and then makes a judgment. This judgment is then sent to our mind as a signal to read. The mind reads it and immediately produces the gut feeling as a reaction, which we literally feel in our lower stomach area.

This all happens before the mind has actually processed the situation for itself to form its own perception, which could be either in alignment or out of alignment with what the heart was telling it.

This is where the confusion comes. We begin overthinking the challenges in our lives, creating scenarios and stories in our heads and clouding our heart's intuition. So there we are with the intuitive "gut" feeling the heart has given us, and at the same time, our mind is overthinking the situation and forming its own judgment of the event. Many times, the two are aligned and the decision is obvious. Other times, they are not.

The general rule is that the more extreme the challenge, the more difficult our decision-making process becomes. Where the heart is leading through our gut and where the mind thinks we should go become further and further apart. This is because there is more riding on higher-level life challenges and our fears are heavily involved in our mind's processing.

So picture the scenario: our heart is leading us to turn right, but our mind is not convinced. It has its guard up, and for one reason or another, it wants to go left. How do we solve this confusion?

Just as they say, listen to your heart, have faith in where it's leading you and start taking action now. The heart will deliver what we want in our lives, which many times is not necessarily what seems logical to our mind in that moment.

Many times, however, our logical mind needs more convincing than only listening to our heart. It wants to understand why the gut disagrees with it before a decision is made. This is what I call conditioning the fit mind. Conditioning your fit mind enables your mind to communicate with your heart's gut feeling by answering this question: "How does listening to my gut feeling benefit my highest values in my life?" or, more specifically, "How does listening to my gut feeling benefit my value #1, value #2 and value #3?" Taking the time to answer this question thoroughly will unveil a massive amount of unexpected value. The heart is never wrong and deserves a wide-open ear.

The heart is connected to the soul and always has the fulfillment of our highest values as its priority, so we must have faith in it. Think of it as your internal protection system. It's our first line of defense. Many times, we talk ourselves out of where the heart's initial intuition is guiding us due to fear. Answering this question with layers upon layers of benefits gives us the knowledge and wisdom to shift our actions more to actions of intuitive faith in our heart.

Understanding this information helps us better see that we actually function at a subconscious level for the large majority of our everyday lives. How? We do it through the heart.

The heart has 100 times the electric current and 5,000 times the magnetic current of the brain. Hence, the electromagnetic field of the heart is much greater than that of the brain. These electromagnetic fields are constantly emitting currents from our bodies for others to pick up and either connect with or become repelled by. What's even crazier is that they have current technology called a SQUID-based magnetometer, which is used to measure extremely subtle magnetic fields and has been able to detect these currents up to three feet away from people in all directions.

This leads us to the law of attraction. Like attracts like. What you think about you bring about. Whether you choose to believe it or not, the law of attraction is happening all around us in every area of our lives at all times. The human body is energy and matter vibrating at a certain frequency depending on where you are in your mindset. The same vibrational currents or "vibes" you emit are then picked up by others and are perceived by them as good or bad based upon their values. They will either be attracted to you or repelled by you because of this.

Our own self-perception is directly responsible for the "vibe" we push out to everyone and everything we come in contact with. The vibe we give off is the product of how fulfilled we are in our lives.

How fulfilled we are is the product of how closely we are living aligned with our highest values.

In the end, the further away we live from our highest values, the less fulfillment we experience and the lower the vibe we produce. The closer we live to satisfy our highest values, the greater the fulfillment and the higher the vibe we produce.

We have all had the memorable event where you walk into a room, meet someone and you are immediately and noticeably either attracted or repelled by them. You were either getting a good vibe or a bad vibe from that person. This phenomenon, which happens subconsciously, is 100% true and a perfect example of our intuitive sense in action. Just as in our "gut feeling" intuitive experience, the heart picks up the electromagnetic vibration a person is giving off, interprets it compared to our highest values in our lives and makes a judgment. This judgment is then sent to our mind as a signal to read. The mind reads it and begins making its own interpretation either in alignment or out of alignment with what the heart was telling it.

What's most amazing is that this happens at a subconscious level without having to think whatsoever. The problem is that most people don't yet have a fit mind. They haven't clearly identified, defined and prioritized their highest values, and because of it, they aren't able to identify specifically how and why different events benefit or challenge what is most important to them. Most simply turn the other cheek and choose to "ignore" it. This leads to a situation where one is left with a lack of knowledge or information, which ironically is the definition of "ignorance". I guess ignorance is not bliss, is it? Remember, you deserve this and the solution starts by taking 20 minutes to complete the Demartini Values Determination process to clearly map your values out. When we do, it gives us the power to clearly understand why we are being directed or led a certain way by the heart.

When you clearly define your highest values, in times of confusion and fear, you can accurately answer the following questions to help you understand your heart's desires with certainty.

If you only see the drawbacks in a situation, answer the question "How does this event / person benefit my highest values?" or, more specifically, "How does this event / person benefit my value #1, value #2 and value #3?" If you only see the benefits in a situation, answer the question "How is this event / person a drawback to my highest values?" or, more specifically, "How is this event / person a drawback to my value #1, value #2 and value #3?"

Answering these questions until you have exhausted all thoughts will provide all the clarity you will need. When our gut feelings don't match what our mind is telling us, confusion is the logical end result. Understanding the situation clears all confusion and brings a level of balance and transparency to our thought patterns. It enables us to be, as Dr. John Demartini says, "quietly grateful for whatever occurs."

In summary, the heart guides us. Educating our mind with knowledge of our values creates an understanding of how and why the heart is responding the way it is. It's guiding us towards the fulfillment of what is most important to us. If we don't have a fit mind, we aren't fully aware of our values and how everything and everyone around us is directly impacting them. We are left disconnected. What's most interesting and almost obvious at this point is that the values of the heart and the mind are exactly the same. What's missing is the mind's recognition of this connection. Connect the dots and endless possibilities are exposed.

I feel Michael Gerber, author of *The E-Myth Revisited*, summed everything up amazingly when he spoke about the passion of the soul and mind working together as one. He said, *"It's the passion of the soul that keeps jumping off rocks, that yearns to fly like a bird; it's the passion of the mind that pursues visions. Without the passion of the mind, the passion of the soul spins out of control chasing first this thing and then that. Without the passion of the soul, however, the passion of the mind creates an endless stream of empty suits, dreams without heart, form without substance. It is the purposeful integration of the two that puts the juice to work in the invention of a great business."*

I will add to this and say that this same integration not only invents a great business, it invents a great life. Without the communication between the two, the soul / heart and the mind become confused and begin to question each other simply because they don't understand each other.

Ask yourself the question "How does the information the heart is telling me benefit my highest values?" It will open the lines of communication and understanding between the heart and the mind.

I always say it's doing the extra 1% that 99% of people aren't willing to do that makes all the difference in life. Taking the time to do this gives us a formal understanding of where the heart is guiding us and, most importantly, why. Completing this exercise during challenging times will give us the information we need to connect the mind and gut feelings.

If you didn't seize the opportunity to complete the Values Determination process compliments of Dr. John Demartini that I spoke of earlier in the book, now is a great time: www.drdemartini.com. This will clearly map out your values for you, leaving you armed and dangerous.

Understanding Your Heart.
Many times our heart tells us one thing and our mind tells us another. This exercise will enable you to connect the two and gain an understanding of why the heart is guiding you left when your mind says to go right.

If you only see the drawbacks in a situation, answer the question "How does this event / person benefit my highest values?" or, more specifically, "How does this event / person benefit my value #1, value #2 and value #3?"

If you only see the benefits in a situation, answer the question "How is this event / person a drawback to my highest values?" or, more specifically, "How is this event / person a drawback to my value #1, value #2 and value #3?"

GOAL BLOCK

"Whatever the mind can conceive and believe it can achieve" is a quote from Napoleon Hill found in his world famous book *Think and Grow Rich*. Whatever you think about you bring about. Yes, we are speaking about the law of attraction. We first create a vision in our minds. Then we build and strengthen the vision as we fine-tune the details of the creation. Finally, we take action moving towards making the vision a reality.

We have all heard of visualization. It truly is a magical and real phenomenon. This enables us to conceive ideas and desires and then bring life to them. The mind is unable to tell the difference between what we dream, what we daydream, and reality. Why is this an incredible advantage for us? Visualizing the creation and accomplishment of your goals in your mind, especially with repetition, activates your cerebral cortex, physiologically enabling your body to ready itself for change. The goal has been visualized as complete and is now as good as done. Your body is ready to make a change, now. All there is to do is have faith and take action now, not later.

So what if I find myself not taking action towards my goals? This is where many people get stuck for a number of reasons. We say we want something in our lives, and then the actions we take say something completely different. Why? Fear of failure, fear of not being good enough and also because most times we fail to identify the big-picture value that accomplishing the goal will bring into our lives. These all lead to hesitation, procrastination, frustration and excuses in our lives.

If we aren't able to identify enough reason and value from what we will be gaining in our lives by crushing the challenges in front of us, the chances of quitting when it becomes difficult increase astronomically. The value of breaking the boundary of the challenge was never created and we in turn set ourselves up for failure when the challenge gets hot or, in many cases, before the battle even begins.

Now, I don't care if this is a fear of public speaking or a fear of family dispute. The only solution to make progress in any situation involving fear is to identify the fear and crush it.

First ask yourself, "What is the fear associated with the challenge you are facing?" Next, ask yourself, "If that fear were to happen, how would it benefit your highest values?" or, more specifically, "If that fear were to happen, how would it benefit your value #1, value #2, and value #3?" We perceive it would only be a drawback in our lives, but we know there is never a front without a back. There is always a polar opposite in all situations.

Now that we've talked about breaking through our fears, let's identify the type of fear we do want. The only fear we must have present in our lives is the fear of not doing our absolute best and fulfilling the standards we have set for ourselves. We must aim for our ideal and not settle for limitation. Instead of letting fear stun our progress, we use the fear to our advantage as a foundation for true courage.

So if it isn't fear, what else could it be? If you are facing a challenging situation that is keeping you stunted in your growth and there aren't any fears associated with a challenge, there may be a disconnect. This is when we say we want something but we actually don't. What I mean by this is that the goals were either a fantasy or they were never our own to begin with.

When we have a fantasy of a situation, we only see the glory that would be brought into our lives. What we fail to identify are the challenges and drawbacks associated with our highest values. There is never a front without a back. There is never an upside without a downside. The reality is that any time we spend away from what is most valuable to us in our lives becomes time spent doing things less valuable to us. This will lead to self-resentment. Why? Because we are failing to take action and nourish what is most valuable to us. The self-resentment is merely a feedback mechanism meant to lead us back to being authentic and honoring the time we choose to dedicate to what we love most in our lives.

Every single person on Earth has the exact same 24-hour period every day to get shit done. Every single person also chooses how they allocate this time. Point being, if we aren't allocating time towards pursuing something we say we want, chances are we don't really want it. Our parents may have assigned us the goal or we may be comparing ourselves to someone else, expecting ourselves to live inside of someone else's highest values. There can never be fulfillment in life attempting to live someone else's life, just as someone else could never find true fulfillment if they were expected to live their life according to their highest values. Remember: "Envy is ignorance, imitation is suicide." The wise words of Ralph Waldo Emerson.

When we compare ourselves to others and fail to honor exactly who we are and what we love, this is when we find we are trying to live the desires of someone else. It may be what our parents wanted for us, or what our spouse or significant other wanted, but not what we want. When this is the case, many times we become rebellious by not taking the actions necessary to advance towards the so-called goal because the desire was never ours to begin with. We inherently reject and sabotage the situation, trying desperately to get back to our authentic self, pursuing what we actually desire for our lives. At the same time, we tend to then beat ourselves up because we aren't doing the things we feel we should be doing. As Tony Robbins says, we begin "shoulding" all over ourselves.

If this is you, my advice is set yourself free and be honest with yourself first and foremost. If others disagree with your decisions, congratulations! Your certainty and leadership are growing. Nobody ever said success and personal growth were easy. The greater the challenge, the greater the reward. If you want to really gain from your challenges, set your goals to the astronomical 10x level, put on your armor, draw your sword and prepare to get after it as if your fulfillment dependent on it because, in all cases, it does.

If you are disconnected with a goal and have no fear associated with what you are pursuing but truly want to make it a part of your life, identifying the massive benefits it will add to what is most important to you in your life will unveil this information to you. To do this, all you have to do is answer the question "How is accomplishing this goal benefiting my highest values?" or, more specifically, "How is accomplishing this goal benefiting my value #1, value #2, and value #3?" If you really desire it and take the time to dig deep with the question past your own denial, stacking benefit upon benefit, you will see the big picture of the massive value in front of you. This massive value will be the fuel needed for you to take the necessary actions to crush your goal.

Dissolving Your Goal Block; Breaking through Fear

The fears we have are nightmares we have created in our minds with the thought that the situation is all bad with zero good to *be had. When we look into the universal law of polarity, we come to find that this is, in fact, impossible. There can never be dark without there being light. Both sides exist in all situations simultaneously. Knowing this, the greatest obstacle in breaking through these fears then becomes ourselves. So let's break the boundary.*

First ask yourself what is the fear associated with a challenge you are facing?

_____

_____

_____

_____

Next, ask yourself, if that fear were to come true, how would that benefit your value #1, value #2, and value #3? (List 25 answers minimum.)

_____

_____

_____

_____

_____

_____

Showing How Your Goals Will Benefit What Is Most Important to You in Your Life

How will accomplishing this goal benefit your value #1, value #2, and value #3? (List 25 answers minimum.)

TAKING MASSIVE ACTION

I didn't intend on dedicating a full chapter to taking massive action, but the truth is that the message it delivers is by far the most important takeaway of this book. There are thousands of personal development programs and books out there with amazing, life-changing content. That said, if it's not applied, it quickly becomes useless. Taking massive action is by far the most critical component needed to accomplish any and every dream that you have. It needed to be highlighted as a standalone.

Without taking massive action, what you say you want will never get done. Yes, we can have all the strategies in the world—a written-down, bullet-proof plan with action steps all outlined right in front of us—but without taking action it becomes irrelevant. So how can we condition ourselves to continually make progress? By using a simple tool designed to prompt immediate action towards our goals. Mel Robbins gives us this easy-to-adopt tool in her book *The 5 Second Rule*.

The 5 Second Rule talks about how we make our decisions as people. Mel explains that we continually talk ourselves out of heart-felt action. She says that from the moment we feel a heart-felt decision, we have five seconds to take massive action, or else we will begin to process the situation in our mind and talk ourselves out of the heart's intuition.

The 5 Second Rule says that the moment you have a heart-felt instinct to take action, count backwards 5, 4, 3, 2, 1, go. Then take immediate physical action on "Go." The counting backwards is a distraction strategy from patterns such as worry, excuses and talking ourselves out of listening to the heart, all of which are based on fear and self-doubt. Counting backwards also helps us focus our attention on what we need to do and prompts us to act. This allows us to break through hesitations and barriers holding us back from maximizing our capacity in all areas of our lives with all challenges.

Ideas and desires are queen here, while action is king. Counting down activates the pre-frontal cortex, preparing our mind for a change. "Go" represents the rocket ship blasting off. This is where we burst into action without any thought. The physical action you take happens at the end of the counting to physiologically initiate a new direction. Before you can even begin to wrap cognition around the decision-making process, your body is already gone and into action. By the time your mind catches up, it simply follows because you are already in motion, committed and decided.

Yes, cognition and thinking through situations is considered a protection mechanism for our own best interest. But is it really? Or is it truly a justification system based upon fear and self-doubt? The choice was made from the heart. The choice was rooted in your innate intuition based on your true desires, ambitions, goals, or whatever you decide to label them. You will be acting on and responding to subconscious instincts tied to the goals most important to you, right from the heart. No fear to blind us, no mind fucks we are all experts with. If you fail to take action within five seconds of an inspired action, your mind takes over along with fear and what we like to call reason. I guess it makes us all feel better that we can blame reason simply because it's much easier than seeing the truth of what our "reason/excuse" has actually disabled and held us back from in our lives.

Svante Arrhenius, a Swedish scientist, introduced the term "activation energy". This is the minimum amount of energy required to begin a reaction. Arrhenius said, "It takes the most energy saved up to start an object or process into motion from a dead stop." Sir Isaac Newton's first law of motion follows up activation energy perfectly, saying, "an object in motion stays in motion with the same speed and in the same direction using less energy, unless it is acted upon by an unbalanced force." But once in motion an object remains in motion with less energy needed and until it is acted upon by another.

Once you count down 5, 4, 3, 2, 1, go, you begin moving and your body has been activated into motion. At this point, the only force that could disrupt your progress is taking your focus off the heart and failing to take massive action towards where it's guiding you. This is the unbalanced force capable of stunning your growth.

"Your feelings don't matter. The only thing that matters is what you DO." Mel Robbins, The 5 Second Rule:

Transform Your Life, Work, and Confidence with Everyday Courage

INFLUENCE: MEETING DR. JOHN DEMARTINI

Let me begin my introduction of Dr. John Demartini by sharing with you the story behind how I was introduced to him.

It was 2009 and I was a full-time school teacher working for Erie One Boces, a vocational technology education center. I had been hired by Erie One to develop the curriculum for its new upcoming personal training program and was now teaching it. The program was developed for juniors and seniors, preparing them to become certified personal trainers by the time they graduated.

I remember it like it was yesterday. I had just finished a great day of teaching and I was writing my lesson on the board for the next day when I received a phone call.

It was my fiancée (now my wife). The conversation began normally by catching up on the day, and then a stick was abruptly thrown in the spokes when she dropped a bomb on me letting me know that she was pregnant. I really don't recall the wording of my initial reaction, but my wife says it was "Holy shit..." I was a bit caught off guard to say the least. What I do remember is thinking how grateful I was that I had proposed to her just one week prior. Talk about good timing. All kidding aside, the fact that I was able to sell myself to my wife has got to be my greatest accomplishment to this date. She means everything to me.

This moment left me awestruck in reflection. There I was working in a field I loved, I had a steady full-time position with great benefits, but the truth was that I was completely unfulfilled. I felt the very low ceiling over my head. It became clear that regardless of how hard I busted my butt, I was restricted in my growth professionally and financially, which quickly became a huge issue for me. My values had shifted 180 degrees and I was brought back to a vision I had created years prior of what I desired for my life and for my future family. I had always envisioned being in a position professionally and financially able to solely support my entire family, creating endless options for us.

At the same time, I had been holding on to the vision of impacting and transforming a million lives with my weight loss solution for the past 12 years as I developed my skillset. For the past five years, I had been denying my dream of one day owning my own facility where I could apply and refine what I wanted to deliver to others. The day after finding out the news, I began taking action. I had no idea what was going to come of it, or how it was going to happen, but I began constructing a business plan for what was to be the beginning of an incredible adventure. There was no more time to waste. In my heart, I felt that the time was now, or the time would be gone, so I took it.

Fast forward six months later and I was ready to launch my first business venture called "Body & Soul Bootcamp" right out of my basement in East Aurora, New York. I was filled with a beautiful combination of fear and excitement. That said, I was committed to doing whatever it took. The stakes had become very real and, for the first time in my life, coming up short was not an option for me. I would crush this and when I fell, I would get up faster and crush it harder.

Within a month, the basement was filled. I was teaching school full-time during the day then coming home and teaching two evening sessions every weekday, along with three sessions on Saturdays. Suddenly, things were going much better professionally and financially, and I remember thinking, *Let's really do this man.*

That month, my dad, my greatest mentor, gave me an incredible opportunity. He offered to loan me the $40,000 I was going to need to open my own facility. I'm forever grateful to my parents for this and I'll never forget it. I began building our first brick-and-mortar location in East Aurora, New York, which was on target to open January 1st, 2010. My plan was to hire a full-time trainer who would train all of the morning sessions every day as I was still teaching. Then I would come in after school and teach the evening sessions, just as I had been doing up to this point. Seemed like a solid plan at the time.

Four weeks before we were scheduled to open, I awoke with a revelation, which, looking back, was a bit of a DUH moment. I had zero processes or systems for the operation of my vision. I had created the entire program in my head over the past 12 years. Nothing was written whatsoever. I remember the feeling when I realized that the product would never be correct if anyone other than me was delivering it and developing a system to replicate the reach of the product. It was absolute terror.

The final takeaway was that either I was going to drop everything and crush this with everything I had or I'd stop construction and shut the doors before I even opened. This was a night of very little sleep.

The next morning was a Tuesday. I remember dropping my things off in my classroom and making my way down to the principal's office. The walk seemed to take forever as my heart literally felt like one constant heartbeat. I reached the principal's office, shut the door and without hesitation let her know that this Friday was going to be my last day of teaching. Let's just say she was about as far away from pleased as you could be. Looking back, I completely agree with the way she felt. I left her in a bind, that was for sure, but for me it went much deeper than that.

What I did know about myself at that point in my life was that I did not want to do anything half-assed. I am either all in or I don't play the game. In the classroom, I was already gone in my mind and on to this next venture. I loved and respected every single one of those kids I was teaching and I recognized that I was doing them a disservice by not giving them everything I had. They deserved someone 100% invested in the program and, more importantly, in them. That was no longer me.

I know I'm making this entire process sound glorious and perfect. Well, the truth is it was anything but. I had no idea what I was getting into, and my actions 100% reflected that.

Looking at the law of polarity, we know that there cannot be a front without a back. In this case, the front was the fact that I was taking massive action towards an amazing opportunity. The back was that I felt I was drowning every minute of every day. I was fumbling and fully exposed for everyone to see and I had no idea how to handle myself. Long story short, I handled it like a fucking baby.

The first year of my brick-and-mortar experience was nearly my last. I had been gifted endless blessings in my life and I disregarded them. In fact, looking back, it seems at that point I didn't even have room for love, gratitude and appreciation. I was filled to the brim with lack and self-pity because of the situation I was in.

At that point in my life, I was a big, angry, resentful, miserable person filled with excuses. I was a boy trying to become a man, but the truth was that I was an entitled man searching for Mommy and Daddy to save me. Not only that, but I was pointing the finger and blaming my situation on those closest to me, rather than appreciating and celebrating the amazing opportunity together. To top it off, I was so stubborn and distracted by feeling sorry for myself that I had become blind to the reality of what was really happening and I couldn't even see it. I had created a monster and I felt alone and out of control. My wife will always be a saint for not kicking me to the curb during this time. I am forever grateful that she was able to believe in me more than I was able to believe in myself. Timing has a mysterious yet perfect way of fitting itself into our lives, doesn't it? Whether my friend Dr. Steve Novelli knew it or not, his timing couldn't have been better. I had created an incredible storm around myself and I needed help.

I remember it like it was yesterday. We were in Taste coffee shop in East Aurora, New York when Steve began teaching me about Dr. John Demartini's work. I knew immediately that this was what I wanted in my life. It became a must for me and I signed up for my first seminar with Dr. Demartini later that night.

For those who have never heard of Dr. John Demartini, I highly recommend checking him out at www.drdemartini.com. He is a performance and human behavior specialist and also considered a polymath, which is "a person of great and varied knowledge of learning."

John began his early life disempowered by his teachers, who told him and his parents that he was less than and would never accomplish anything. He was labeled dyslexic and never read a book in his life until he was 17 years old after meeting his greatest mentor, Paul Bragg. After one evening with Paul, John's life would never be the same. He became empowered and his growth and development exploded from that point on.

Since then, John has read well over 29,000 books, initially beginning a career as a doctor of chiropractic and soon shifting his energy to his love, which is speaking, writing, teaching and traveling the world. Today, John continues his worldwide mission of helping others maximize their potential and love their lives.

I (and I would say all others who have had the pleasure of meeting and/or studying under Dr. Demartini) consider him one of the greatest minds of this century.

The first event I attended was in Houston, Texas, called "The Breakthrough Experience", which is one of Dr. Demartini's main programs he delivers throughout the world. As I entered the room, I was at a point in my life where I was struggling with the transition into entrepreneurship. I was lost and out of control. I was scared, felt insignificant and I was challenged more than I had ever been in my life.

My relationship with my wife was failing. My presence as a father was negligent at best. My self-perception was that I was incapable. My mission was unclear because it hadn't been defined. I was socially withdrawn because I was failing and I was ashamed. I was financially in a hole. I was new to entrepreneurship and was searching for a handout rather than doing the work and crushing it. Oh, and my fit body was being neglected.

It all came together for me in a moment that first day of the program. I was asked the simple but transformative question, "What would you rather be doing? Because you don't have to do what you are doing if you are miserable." Suddenly, it all came together for me. I was struck with the realization that I would rather be doing nothing but exactly what I was doing with my life. It was and had been a choice the entire time and, up until that point, I had not realized it. All I had been able to concentrate on was the fact that I had no idea what I was doing. The reality was that my own fear was blinding me and I was dragging the life I loved along with those I loved most through the mud.

What it comes down to is that I was afraid of others seeing me fail, not realizing failing is vital to mastering my life. In fact, failing is "the" necessity in order to master anything. The quicker we run towards failure, the quicker we will learn to master the challenge and grow. Well, that and applying what we learned from all of our falls and doing it consistently over and over again. Now I embrace unfamiliar territories, running towards them headfirst with a ready-aim-fire mentality. I take action to the best of my ability now and put the rest of the puzzle together as I go.

My life completely changed that day. It was the day I gained a new level of love and respect for my wife and for myself. This changed everything instantly and has only grown since. During the program, Dr. Demartini introduced us to the Values Determination process he created. This is a process showing us individually what we hold most dear to us in our lives and it ultimately explains why we do what we do.

I left the program with a different perspective of everyone around me. I now had genuine love and appreciation for others and what they hold as most important to them in their lives. Every single person is unique and extraordinary in their own way. I quickly realized that expecting others to live outside of their own personal values defies universal law. I'm forever grateful to John. The knowledge he delivered ultimately saved my marriage and my family life, catapulted my career and shifted all areas of my life.

As I left this program, I decided I needed to spend more time around this man.

Since then, I've attended seven live seminars spanning the equivalent of 28 15-hour days' worth of classroom training with John. I've purchased every one of his 24 CD sets and DVDs and devoured each of them a minimum of three times.

I became a certified Demartini Method facilitator and have since adopted and integrated this work into my own company as an integral part of our culture and all of our services, helping thousands of people and the number is growing every day. My dream of one million will be here in no time.

I don't tell you this to brag. I tell you because I became obsessed. My values changed and I became obsessed with mastering my emotions, my actions, my reactions, my life, my relationships with people around me, and my ability to best serve others, which I've come to learn is a life-long process of continual growth. I became obsessed with the idea that what I had dreamed about for years was right there if I was only willing to step up and own the continual process of challenge, failure and triumph.

Every day I use this work in my own life and the lives of those I serve. It empowers me because the growth is vast and constant. The deeper you go, the more you discover and unveil. What I found through this education experience is that in order to best serve others around you, there is the absolute need to take care of your own growth and development first and foremost, mentally as well as physically. Then and only then will you be prepared to put your best foot forward in all situations.

This is where I found my love and appreciation for constant education. The value it brought into my life was enlightening. It inspires me and, just like eating, I do it every day. It's about more than survival—it's essential for my thrival. If that isn't a word, well, I just made it one.

As I built my knowledge and applied Dr. Demartini's principles into my life, it became very clear to me that this work was something that could provide a massive amount of value to the experience I was providing my clients. Reaching a body transformation goal and keeping the results has been a very challenging battle for many people because there has never been a clear system enabling people to see the value they would be adding to their lives by building a fit body.

This was what was missing and I was certain if I could figure out how to implement this, it would change the game for my guests and the weight loss industry as a whole.

This system would enable me to show each individual how transforming their fit body would directly benefit what is most important to them in their lives, their highest values. This has never been communicated with a clear, individualized system in the weight loss industry to my knowledge.

Yes, there are generic methods of goal-setting and asking people their why, but this was failing me and those I was serving. I needed something that would show them specifically what would change for them in their own lives. Something that would build such an incentive that they would complete the exercise, get changed into workout clothes, get to our facility and start because they couldn't wait to get to the other side.

Here's the big picture. It's not about the goal itself. It's not about losing the 50 pounds. It's about what will be enabled in our lives once we achieve the goal of losing 50 pounds. It's about how what is most important to us will benefit from losing the 50 pounds. Losing the weight is simply a means of achieving what we want. This system I've created using my work, along with the work of Dr. Demartini and many others, lays this entire picture out in front of us, making what's at stake and also what's available to us as clear as day.

I see so many focusing on the fact that their doctors told them they should lose weight because they are overweight according to the BMI chart or that they need to lose weight because they are pre-diabetic and showing progressive signs of heart disease. I don't know about you, but that sounds about as inspiring as eating a box of nails.

Honestly, for some people, this is exactly what they need to hear to change direction and make it happen. For most, however, it only buries the hatchet deeper, making them feel helpless and even hopeless. Let's face it, losing 30, 50, 100 or 200 pounds is a challenge requiring a massive amount of inspiration, determination, action and consistency. Most of us need profound reasons much more specific to us than just our health to feel the light switch go off. Most of us need to see exactly how losing the weight and getting the fit body will impact what is most important to us in our lives. This is what matters most to us as individuals.

Dr. Demartini said, "The quality of your life is based upon the quality of the questions that you ask." I love this because it not only holds true for the relationships we build with others but also the relationship we build with ourselves. This quote was my focus as I went through the process of creating the transformation discovery system made to deliver effective and lasting weight loss. The system is a combination of the Demartini Values Determination process, my original goal-setting system, and sections of The Demartini Method that I extracted and customized specifically for my program.

Let me ask you, when was the last time you listed a specific goal you have in your life then answered the question "How will accomplishing this goal benefit my highest values?" or, more specifically, "How will accomplishing this goal benefit my value #1, value #2, and value #3?" Not a difficult process at all, but if you are like most, the answer ironically is that you can't remember, or simply never. Not a problem because today is a different day. Coming up, you will have the opportunity to determine your highest values directly through Dr. Demartini's website as well as completing my transformation discovery system.

Why would we want to take the time out of our busy lives to do something like this? Let me ask you a question. If you really want what you say you want, do you think it's important to ask yourself why you want it? Of course. The challenge is that many times when we simply ask ourselves why, we give a general surface answer. Yes, it sounds good and it's meaningful, but what if you could amass a series of profound whys that would leave you in awe, inspiring you to start fast and finish strong every single day even once you already hit your goal? Would that interest you? Of course, this is an obvious question with an obvious answer. The answers you give during the transformation discovery exercise will create this series of whys through what is called the sum of one or many.

The sum of one or many is a law explaining how value is created for, and also extracted from, our lives through one extremely significant event or the sum of many small events. As you go through the transformation discovery exercise using your fit body goals we identify, you will find that, for some goals, the value you will create in your heart will happen in small jumps consisting of several answers, while other goals will uncover significant benefits with very few answers needed to create a high level of value.

Overall, my objective with adding this component to my business was showing people the big picture about what attaining their fit body was all about. Besides the fit body itself, I wanted them to gain the perspective of what the fit body really would be adding to what is most important to them in their lives. I wanted to create more value in pushing through the challenges along the way until the goal is reached. I wanted to empower people with the wisdom needed to see the value in keeping their goals once they were reached and this is exactly what I've done.

The best part about the entire process in my opinion is that it's simple and extremely powerful. If you dig in and really take the time, the amount of value you will receive will create a cause, drive and a level of inspiration much greater than you ever expected. Why? Because it's real. You will see it and, most importantly, you will feel it.

Personally, I've found so much value with Dr. Demartini's work that we've infused sections of The Demartini Method into our hiring process. What I do know is that the strength of a company is only as good as its team. That said, in order to make sure we get the right team, there are two crucial steps we now take. First, we find out the highest values of what is most important to every potential team member we interview. Second, we ask them the question "How does helping us accomplish our mission of transforming lives nationally benefit your value #1, value #2, and value #3?"

Many people are just looking for a job. Personally, I am not looking for those people. To provide a superior experience for those we serve without having to micromanage our team, it's crucial we find people who are attached to the same mission that we are. If we aren't able to add massive value to our team members' lives through their involvement in helping us achieve our mission, it isn't the right fit for either of us and we move on. It absolutely must be a win-win situation. This helps prevent us from hiring the wrong people and saves us from future headaches.

Fit Body Free Writing

Take five minutes to answer the following question. "How does transforming and getting a fit body benefit my highest values?" or, more specifically, "How does transforming and getting a fit body benefit my value #1, value #2, and value #3?"

_____

_____

_____

OUR HIGHEST VALUES

The study and practice of human values is believed to span all the way back to the times of the ancient Athenian philosophers Plato and Aristotle, both born several hundred years BC. Many speculate it was even earlier than that.

Human values all begin with the study of axiology, which is the study of human values and worth. Through my studies of human behavior and potential, I've learned our value structures explain why we are driven towards every action in our lives. Our values determine the way we perceive, act on, react to and filter every situation in our existence. Our values are in fact our identities.

Every person, no matter what race or color, has a 100% unique, prioritized set of values that they live by. In fact, no two people have the same values structure. This is according to quantum physics and the Pauli exclusion principal stating that no two people view the universe the same way and therefore no two have the exact same values structure.

There has actually been an experiment proving this. We all have what is 1st most important, 2nd most important, 3rd most important, 4th most important and so on value in our lives. These are prioritized in our minds, and our life demonstrates these values every second of every day in what we think about, what we daydream about, what we talk about, how we spend our money, how we spend our time, what and who we surround ourselves with, where we are most reliable, disciplined, focused and organized, what we visualize, what inspires us, and what goals we set most consistently for ourselves. These are considered our highest values, our hierarchy of values, or simply what is most important to us in our lives.

As people, we set unrealistic expectations of others and ourselves. We expect ourselves to conform and live inside of someone else's value structure. At the same time, we expect others to live inside of our values structure when they don't see something our way.

We all perceive the world based on our values. Events happen every day and these are neither good nor bad, they just are. Our mind unconsciously labels the situations as good or bad based on our values. Does it threaten our personal values of what we love? It's bad. Does it support our personal values of what we love? It's good. The interesting thing is that many times two different people perceive the same situation the opposite way. One sees good, the other bad. So who's right? They both are. Who's to say one's values are more important than another's? And when you have an answer to who is right in a situation, it's just because you have a value set closer to the person you sided with.

We judge based on our values. We judge based on our emotions, we judge based on our insecurities. If we are not at our physical best, how can we have the certainty in ourselves? If we don't have certainty in ourselves, how can we accept that what we see in others and that which we deny in us is in fact a direct reflection of our disowned parts? According to the universal law of reflection, this is exactly what it is. There are roughly 4,260 human traits, and every single person possesses both sides of all traits to an equal degree. Denying this is denying ourselves.

If we aren't physiologically conditioned, how can our bodies be in a position to take us to new heights? That's just it, they can't. Without this peak conditioning, are we best prepared to process information clearly and quickly? Are we in a position to have the best judgment of ourselves? If not, do you feel we may be biased or less favorable to some more than others? How can we best form a judgment and perceive if we aren't physically prepared to do so? Either we are prepared or we are not. Of course, there are varying degrees of this, but the reality is that either we are moving forward and thriving or we are not. There is no in between.

Interestingly, the large majority of people couldn't tell you their exact values structure accurately. That said, what's important to note is that this is what we live by and display nonetheless, even if we perceive it not to be. What many of us tend to do through our own personal development is inject others' values into our lives in the form of either social expectations we are trying to follow and conform to or the display of another individual's personal values reflected through areas of our lives we don't yet have complete ownership over or empowerment in.

We say we should, we need to, we have to do particular things in life in order to fill areas that society or others say are necessary, but then we don't do them and we do something different because that isn't really what we want to do. Then what happens? We begin beating ourselves up for not fulfilling this false idealism. Why is it false? This is only what society or other individuals project onto us. We then inject these values due to a lack of confidence and empowerment in certain areas of our lives. It doesn't enable us to be true and appreciative of our own individual values system, which, when embraced, enables us to maximize our capacity. It puts us in a position to conform, leading to resentment of ourselves.

An important note worth repeating is that, according to universal law, we can never expect ourselves or any others to be fulfilled while living according to any structure other than our own individual values structure in life. We all want to live a life working towards fulfilling what is most important to us individually. Expecting others to live within our values structure only sets us up for disappointment and sets false expectations of others in their own quest.

"Love is composed of a single soul inhabiting two bodies."

Aristotle

THE SEVEN AREAS OF LIFE

There are several different models outlining the differing areas of life. The model I'm going to be referring to here is a model used by Dr. Demartini and Zig Ziglar called "the 7 areas of life."

According to this model, there are seven areas of life we all possess and partake in daily. Every person has varying needs and desires in all of these areas. As individuals, we prioritize some areas of life as more important or more "valuable" than other areas.

The seven areas of life in no particular order are: Spiritual, Mental, Financial, Familial, Vocational, Social and Physical.

The spiritual area is your belief in God, or however you choose to define that. Personally, I see spirituality as the belief that we are all here on this earth for a particular set of reasons. The level that we become aware of, and also the more we act accordingly to these particular reasons, the more we grow and become aligned with our spirituality. I have found that the closer I am in line with my purpose, the greater my spiritual fulfillment becomes.

The mental area of life is the fit mind and is all about personal growth and development. Of course, this includes development through many forms such as reading, writing and creating. What it really comes down to, however, is our self-perception, defining what is most important to us in our lives, known as our highest values, and understanding how everything we choose to do or not do directly impacts these same values.

Financial is about the amount of value we are able to bring to others. Yes, it is about investment portfolios, money management, personal wealth building, real estate, savings, what's in our bank accounts and a vast number of other categories. However, what it really comes down to is the monetary potential we have at any given moment based on the level of contribution and value we are able to give others. The better prepared and developed we become, the greater we are able to contribute to others. The greater our contribution to others, the greater we will be compensated for it. The greater we are compensated, the greater our opportunity to contribute at an even higher level to an ever-growing number of people. This same cycle repeats infinitely.

Familial includes your immediate and extended family relationships in your life.

Vocational is your work, career or any hobbies you are involved with, contributing to your livelihood.

Social is your active involvement with your friends and others you associate with in social settings, personally as well as professionally.

Finally, the physical area of life is the fit body. This is our commitment to practicing all aspects of health, including but not limited to nutrition and exercise.

> *"We must let go of the life we have planned, so as to accept the one that is waiting for us."*
>
> *Joseph Campbell*

FIT MIND + FIT BODY

You may be wondering, *Can I have a fit mind and a fit life without a fit body?*

Sure you can have a fit mind and a semi-fit life without a fit body. It just depends on whose standards you are comparing it to and the level of value you want to add into your life. Regardless, it becomes impossible to truly maximize your capacity of the fit life when the body responsible for performing everything involved in attaining the fit life isn't maximized itself. What some may define as a fit life others may define as unfit. A fit life is all in the eyes of the beholder. However we define it, in order to have a fit life, we must first master our fit mind.

Having a fit mind will not only affect one area of life, it will have massive impact in all areas. Why? When you have a fit mind, you are always armed with the ability to question how every situation, person or event directly impacts what is most important to you in your life. If we don't have a fit mind and haven't specifically and accurately defined our own highest values, this immediately becomes impossible and all that is left is inaccuracy and speculation.

Our personal values directly affect how we perceive everything in the world. The only way we can dominate this process is through defining our values and learning how to ask quality questions about the situations, people and events in our lives. Is it good or bad? Does it have massive benefits with a high level of support to our highest values, or are there massive drawbacks and challenges with our highest values? This is having a fit mind.

Tony Robbins said, "The greatest leaders are those who are able to master their emotions." When it comes down to it, our emotions represent a single-sided polarized perception of a situation. It's seeing one side without the other. It is seeing it as only good or only bad, which the universal law of polarity shows us does not exist. This is exactly what the fit mind delivers. It allows us to see and understand the other side when we are unable. It enables us to process and make sense of what the heart is communicating to us when we just can't see it.

When we feel threatened, many times we feel irrational in our decision-making and our choice of words. The reason is because of our uncertainty involved with the situation at hand. We try rationalizing the event and become confused. The reason is because we have nothing to specifically rationalize with. We haven't defined our personal values hierarchy on paper and therefore don't have the ability to gain a true understanding of the impact choosing to go left or right will have on what is most valuable to us in our lives.

In order to gain this perspective, we must specifically define our personal values hierarchy. Then and only then will we have our individualized foundation always ready to answer the quality questions necessary to deliver us certainty in our everyday decision-making processes.

If you are struggling with committing yourself to defining your values and attaining a fit mind, ask yourself how having a fit mind will benefit you in all seven areas of life and answer it vigorously until you have a minimum of 30 answers total. This will unlock the extreme value that resides here for all of us.

This consists of answering the questions "How will having a fit mind benefit you spiritually?" "How will having a fit mind benefit you mentally?" and "How will it benefit you financially, familially, vocationally, socially, and physically?" until you have thoroughly answered these questions with all seven areas of life. Overall, this experience will give you a higher level of awareness of the gifts and massive value a fit mind brings to your life.

Now take everything we just talked about and imagine your entire body is in a more accelerated, physiologically stronger high-efficiency state. Let me ask you, is there any way all areas of life wouldn't also become drastically more accelerated, stronger and more efficient as well?

Would you agree that if you were to prime everything you do by achieving a fit body you would be positioned to do everything better? When you master your body and achieve a fit body, you maximize the ability of all 100 trillion cells in the human body. Physiologically everything just fires at a whole new level in all areas of your life. That said, it's impossible down to a cellular level not to better your best with a fit body.

Spiritually, a fit body positions us with a more capable and maximized body to carry out our visions and fulfill our purpose more passionately and with a higher level of energy.

Mentally, the simple shift in our confidence explodes all other areas of life due to the ripple effect. We view ourselves as a better version of ourselves, and we exude this in all situations. The "vibe" we emit changes and becomes more appealing and attractive to everyone and everything we come in contact with.

Financially and vocationally, we position ourselves to achieve greater success. The fit body physiologically enhances our electromagnetic vibration and therefore the signals we give off to others. Our enhanced confidence alone gives us the ability to speak up where we normally would not and to approach people or put ourselves in situations that we otherwise would not, just to name a few things. One of these ideas alone is powerful enough to cause massive transformation financially, vocationally and in any area of our lives quite frankly.

Familially, we become a more capable leader. We gain more energy to contribute to our families. The time we spend becomes more focused and of higher quality. We lead by example, showing the massive benefits the fit body delivers in life, which is directly picked up by our family and others we surround ourselves with through what is called attachment bonding. Attachment bonding explains the fact that all of us learn through what we see others do, not what others tell us to do.

Socially, we become more comfortable with ourselves, allowing us to be more transparent. This enables us to attract more of those we desire to surround ourselves with in our lives organically.

Physically, we become the proud owner of a more efficient and effective body to carry out everything we desire in our lives.

Of course, this is a speculative list of possibilities. That said, what I've written is merely a fractionalized sample or tip of the iceberg perspective of what really happens when we own the fit body because when we do, it becomes real. Reading about it is powerful. Applying and experiencing it for yourself immediately makes the experience profound.

Let me ask you a couple of questions. Did anything I listed above resonate with you? Do you feel that attaining any of these experiences would add to the fulfillment of what is most important to you in your life?

Damn right it would. In fact, it is virtually impossible not to have massive shifts upwards in your performance and therefore your fulfillment in all areas of your life. Every cell is stronger, more conditioned, more nourished, more capable and, most importantly, clear and focused on what is most important to you. It is at your full service because it doesn't have to utilize its energy attempting to heal and recover from nutritional abuse and the lack of exercise, which together are a great hindrance to us being able to truly maximize our capacity in all areas of life.

Now, if all I said you had to do to attain this was earn a fit body, would that excite you? If you said no, go ahead and close the book and come back when you are ready. If you said yes, congratulations because it's literally that simple.

As soon as you make the choice in your mind and shift in your actions towards attaining your fit body, everything changes. It's a perfect example of cause and effect. Your entire vibrational energy shifts upward into high gear, impacting every area of your life as an overlapping unit where a jump in one area automatically leads to a jump in other areas. The initial jump in the one area of life was the cause, and the effect is the jump in other areas of life that was caused by the initial jump. This is similar to how compound interest works with investments.

Consider the single example of how gaining the fit body results in a shift in our mental confidence. This alone then leads to transformation in every other area of our life. Now add all the other benefits that will be pouring into your life and you have a phenomenon that is nothing short of magic.

Yes, you can acquire a fit mind, which alone will lead to a semi-fit life, but achieve a fit body and everything is amplified, accelerated and launched into a new quantum.

The Next Level through Communication

Is there another level to this? There is always another level and the next level is mastering your communication skills. This consists of learning others' values then communicating with them inside of their own values structure. It comes down to genuinely showing love and appreciation to everyone for exactly who they are and what they hold dearest to them. Failing to do so is a direct reflection of our own discomfort with who we are as an individual. In other words, failing to do so shows insecurity in our own beliefs.

> *"If you have a limited vocabulary, you will also have a limited vision and a limited future."*
>
> *Jim Rohn*

There are many components we can embrace to enhance our ability to best communicate with others, including but not limited to continually acquiring vast knowledge to speak about. Learning how to speak well in front of individuals and groups. Being sincere with those we are communicating with. Learning to become very brief and clear with our message. Developing a distinct and unique style of how we communicate. Developing a diverse and ever-expanding vocabulary. If you think about it, the greater our vocabulary, and the better we are at expressing it, the more versatile we become in communicating with all types of people of varying cultures, values and interests.

Rohn compared how a lack in education and vocabulary is like trying to see the world while looking through the knothole in a fence. I love this analogy. The more you expand the hole in the fence, the greater your view of the world.

What it comes down to is the fact that it's not what we say, it's all about how we say it. It's important for all of us to understand that every single person perceives things differently according to their highest values. Being empathetic and respectful of others' points of view is the acknowledgement and consideration of others' values due to the fact that perception is reality. If we are truly interested in understanding another point of view, then it doesn't matter what we think about the situation. It matters that we respect what they think and feel. Doing so breaks down the barriers of defense.

No, you don't have to agree with someone else's point of view. It's a matter of respecting them enough to recognize that their viewpoints and opinions are constructed based upon what is most important to them in their lives. This is a true reflection of love and acceptance, and every single person wants to be loved and appreciated for exactly who they are.

So the question surfaces, "Why wouldn't we want to battle to win an argument over what we believe in?" Let me ask you what happens when you dominate and win an argument? Do you really win? Does anyone really win the argument?

If you dominate and win an argument, how does the other person feel: empowered or disempowered? Most of us would agree that we are here with the desire to serve others. We want to inspire, empower, and add value to people's lives—a clear definition of the golden rule. Do unto others as we would have them do to us.

Taking the time to understand people's personal values enables us to take this is a step further by treating others how they want to be treated. This is what I referred to before as the platinum rule and it is only possible if we take the time to truly understand and appreciate what others value in their lives.

So, when is the absolute best time to have and win an argument? Never.

The answer to mastering this situation is showing sincere appreciation, respect and understanding for another's perspectives and opinions.

One simple statement changes everything in these situations. "I understand completely and if I were you in this situation, I would feel the exact same way you do." Why? Because it's true. They perceive the situation a certain way. And if you were in fact them, you would feel the exact same way as they do.

Knowing this fact enables us to display authentic and transparent empathy to others without violating our own point of view. They both exist at the same time, and they are both correct. Who's to say that one person's values are more important than another's? The difference is in the eye of the perceiver. Many people will have different opinions than us. Expecting others to conform to our way of thinking is expecting others to be fulfilled living outside of their highest values. This is impossible and, even if initiated, will most certainly not end well.

This course of action enables others to naturally let their guard down and become more open to listening to your point of view because they realize their viewpoints were listened to and respected.

After the initial response, it's then time to transition and add in the facts behind why you believe the way you do. "I understand completely and if I were you in this situation, I would feel the exact same way you do. Whenever I look at these situations, I always like to gather and study what we know about X." Then add in the facts that you have learned about the topic, along with why you believe what you believe. "I have learned X, which is why I believe X."

The mind connecting with the body gives us the greatest return on investment for all other areas of our lives. The heart leads and intuitively is connected to the soul or the root of our fulfillment. This root is our highest values or what is most important to us in our lives.

If our mind doesn't have clear communication with and faith in the intuitive sense of the heart through understanding and clearly defining our highest values, there will be a lack in alignment and cooperation along with confusion when the two are in communication with each other. Why? We won't be in a position to ask ourselves the quality questions that matter most at that time. "How does following where the heart is guiding me benefit my highest values?" or, more specifically, "How does following where the heart is guiding me benefit my value #1, value #2, and value #3?"

The body is referring to all roughly 100 trillion cells that make up the human body. In short, conditioning our bodies through clean nutrition and short sessions of intense exercise literally transforms us physiologically down to a cellular level. Every cell of the body becomes enhanced, accelerated and more capable in its abilities; this alone leads to a complete shift upwards in our ability to maximize our capacity.

Take, for example, the simple boost mentally in our own self-perception and confidence. Suddenly, everything changes because we approach everything differently. Just from this one simple shift, every other area of life begins to transform and continues to accelerate in its transformation in alignment with your body transformation progress.

If you are not able to see the value that transforming your body will have on what is most valuable to you in your life, you haven't taken the time to thoroughly answer the question. To create strong enough reason for you to invest the effort necessary to transform and make it happen, you must answer the question deeply enough to create a strong enough reason for you. "How does transforming and getting a fit body benefit my highest values?" or, more specifically, "How does transforming and getting a fit body benefit my value #1, value #2, and value #3?"

Of course, in our everyday pursuits, we are inundated with the opinions of others ranging from our friends and acquaintances to our doctors. These are the values and expectations of others speaking. This is what society has set as a standard. Yes, they deserve respect and acceptance. At the same time, what's most important is that we focus on taking actions that are going to give us the greatest benefits to our highest values, in the least amount of time in the most efficient way. Then and only then will we reach the point where we are being true to ourselves.

Failing to do so will result in self-resentment and, eventually, a revolt bringing us back to our most authentic self. In other words, we can only fake it for so long until we just can't take it anymore. At that time, we quickly find our way back to what we organically desire in our lives and begin taking action.

At the end of the day, it really has nothing to do with the goal itself. It's about what will be enabled in our lives once we reach our goals. The goal is purely a strategy to help us get what we really want.

Having a fit mind enables us to answer the question "How does accomplishing *my goal* benefit my highest values?" This creates a foundation of reason, focus and massive value, preparing us to conquer any goals we have in our lives.

If we aren't armed with a fit mind, we miss out.

Taking the Time to Define Your Highest Values

If our mind doesn't have clear communication with and faith in the intuitive sense of the heart through understanding and clearly defining our highest values, there will be a lack in alignment and cooperation along with confusion when the two are in communication with each other. Why? We won't be in a position to ask ourselves the quality questions that matter most at that time. "How does following where the heart is guiding me benefit my highest values?"

Take at least five minutes to answer the following question. How will having a fit mind benefit you spiritually? How will having a fit mind benefit you mentally? How will it benefit you financially? How will it benefit your family? How will it benefit you vocationally? How will it benefit you socially? How will it benefit you physically? Answer these until you have thoroughly answered this question with all seven areas of life.

Overall, this experience will give you a higher level of awareness of the gifts and massive value a fit mind brings to your life.

MY STORY: PART 2

So there I was on a beautiful Saturday afternoon in August. I had just finished my work for the weekend and it was time to rest with the family and have some time for reflection—a perfect time to blow off some steam with a ride on the ATV.

I remember thinking to myself how pumped I was with my own personal development. Just that morning I had hit my fit body goal and everything else in my life as far as I would allow myself to see was awesome.

I was having a cocky moment and I was about to get knocked down a peg.

As I came around the bend, my eyes targeted the jump in the middle of the trail. The same jump I had gone over thousands of times before. This time, I would not be so successful. Approaching it, I realized that the trail was not the same size it was just weeks prior. We had just built a new tree house in our back woods and one of the stilts of the front porch was now sitting directly in the middle of my trail. I quickly thought, *I can thread the needle.*

Apparently, I was having an "I'm unbreakable" moment.

As I launched off the jump and into the air, I immediately knew I was in trouble. The angle I was forced to go off the jump tossed my ATV off the jump at an unexpected angle right towards a tree.

I reacted as quickly as I could, throwing the ATV away from me, but it wasn't fast enough. I was only half off. Smack. The

ATV smashed into the tree and sent me flying like Superman, or maybe not so Superman-like into the air. I landed about 20 feet away hands first and then slid onto my chest.

Now, I'm not making excuses, but the tree got in my way. I quickly assessed the situation, finding a severely shattered left wrist, and was immediately stuck with fear. I remember thinking, *I can't work out. I'm going to gain all my weight back. How am I going to be a leader in the fitness arena if I'm not fit myself?*

Then I broke the boundary of my fear by asking the quality question that changed my life yet again in that moment. "How does this accident benefit my highest values in my life?" or, more specifically, "How does this accident benefit my value #1 my family, my value #2 finance and business expansion, and my value #3 exercise and nutrition?"

The answers I came up with in short were that I was going to spend more time developing my relationship with my family as number one. Secondly, I would now have the time to dig deep into studying finance and business expansion to take my vision to the next level. Thirdly, I committed to extensively studying and applying new nutrition strategies and disciplines into my regimen to make sure I would not relapse to my overweight past history.

As soon as I went through how it benefited what was most important to me, I was clear. I kid you not. I was good with the situation. I knew due to the shape of my wrist that I needed surgery and that I would be pretty useless in many regards for at least a couple days. It was movie time and I was looking forward to sitting back, reflecting and watching some inspirational stuff while I was on painkillers. Yes, I know. Not the most inspirational first step in my upcoming explosive plan, but, to be honest, it was where I was putting my focus to take my mind off my fucked-up body. That said, when it came time for the movies, I decided to do what I do best. Make the experience enjoyable but productive. I watched one movie then one documentary, back and forth. I crushed that time.

When I went to get up off the ground, I realized I hadn't only severely broken my left wrist but also my right index hand as well. I couldn't take off my helmet. Normally, that would be fine, but considering the current circumstance, my body was beginning to go into shock and I was extremely nauseous. So picture it, I'm walking from our backyard towards the house trying to get my wife Laura's attention without the kids knowing their poppa was a mess and, at the same time, not blowing chunks all over my helmet and face.

Not my best moment ... or was it?

Honestly, it was one of the most empowering personal breakthroughs of my life. I had just minutes ago had one of the most important things in my life stripped away from me (which was exercise for the time being), found out how it benefitted what else is most important to me in my life, come up with a plan of action greater and more ambitious than I had the ability to achieve before the accident, and was literally excited to get started on the next step. It was the first time I was able to test the fit mind to that degree.

As I began walking back to my house, I realized what I had just done and that it actually worked. I truly was all good with what had just happened. I remember cracking a smile and actually saying to myself out loud, "Holy shit, it worked," immediately followed by extreme concentration not to upchuck all over my helmet and face.

As a side note, as I went through the exercise while still on the ground, the further I got into it, the less noticeable the pain became. Yes, it sucked for sure, but I am certain it would have been much different had I had an unfit mind.

So I was able to identify how the accident benefited my highest values at the time, but did that value hold steady throughout my experience? Well, for the first year, yes it did. I was in great spirits and holding strong with what I was focusing on.

Looking back at my family life before the accident, my time with them was many times interrupted and lacking focus. I was out of balance from where I wanted to be mostly due to fear. Not the fear of failure but more the fear of success. I was almost distracting myself with fillers that were taking time away from my family and at the same time not allowing me to expand my company's impact close to the pace I desired. I was stalling. What I said I wanted for my life was not matching what I was spending my time on.

I feared how things in my life would change, which ironically is actually what I wanted. I said I wanted to take my life to the next level but wasn't taking the action necessary to do so. Would I have new challenges I didn't expect to come with the growth? Of course. Would I potentially part ways in some relationships along the way? Yup. Would I fall flat on my face? Absolutely, and if I didn't, I would make damn sure I did. Success without failure is nonexistent. These were the fears I was facing.

It was time to change that and make sure my actions were fully aligned with what is most important to me in my life. I realized I wasn't fulfilled. Now I know it's because I was hesitating and battling with what my heart knew the entire time.

I thank God for the fit mind because without it I would have personally crashed hard immediately after the accident. If I hadn't had a fit mind, I would never have been able to interpret and find the benefits of the situation to what is most important to me in my life.

My Studies after the Accident

Before the accident, where I was personally, financially and business development-wise was just fine. I was very blessed to be in a position where I was able to provide for my family on a single income, and my business was very successful.

The accident gave me the opportunity to open and research new resources I never would have imagined accessing beforehand.

I began extensively studying finance and business expansion strategies, leading me to the decision to franchise my company. This is where I found my newfound understanding and appreciation for what stronger finances provided. It all comes down to the potential opportunities it provides us.

For most of my life, I had an issue with money. I always visualized and desired to have monetary access, yet I persecuted myself for the same thoughts. I thought if you desired to be or were financially successful, it was somehow a bad thing and that people would resent it, frown upon it, hate on it, or whatever it was. While all of this may be true, I got over this thinking once I realized my purpose was on hold because of the fact that I was in many ways denying the gift of money.

What I came to realize about money is that it is a tool to unlock opportunities. It has the potential to help us give our visions and dreams legs. I now know that I wasn't taking action because of two things. The fear of what others would think of me and because I didn't know why I desired it. My heart had been pushing me towards it, but I wasn't able to understand it because I hadn't taken the time to ask how having that money would help me accomplish my goals and personal mission. I was in a position where I felt as though I didn't deserve it and this very thinking was putting my dreams on hold.

I have very big dreams. I dream of transforming lives by helping millions break boundaries and lose millions of pounds. When I asked myself, *How am I going to do that?* the only answer was that I needed very strong financial resources and even stronger financial control to make this dream a reality. I had a concept and I was practicing it vigorously. Now, to take my vision to the next level, it became clear that investing in my company to tighten things up and then replicating it to further my impact was a must.

My own personal discovery was that my heart was calling for this and I denied myself of it until I realized that in order to serve more people and have a greater impact, I must have a greater flow of financial resources. It became something I immediately saw as a crucial strategy necessary to create the vision I had dreamed of creating since I was 16 years old. Yes, I had studied finance to a certain extent up to this point but not to the level where I wanted to become a real player in the industry. This was a different ball game and I clearly had work to do.

Through further studies, I quickly began viewing money as exactly what it is—opportunity. Opportunity to do more, serve more, and transform more lives with inspired solutions. Money is something I'm no longer afraid to earn or lose. It's something I now see as a means necessary to accomplish my dream of impact and live the life I envision.

Finance is nothing more than a form of exchange for the products and/or services we provide others. The amount of value we provide others with these products and services is directly proportionate to the monetary gain we accumulate because of it. The more value we provide, the more money we are given to further invest in our efforts, leading to even greater impact potential. Inspiring stuff for sure.

When it comes to nutrition and exercise, before the accident, my regimen was consistent and dead on point. The issue was that I had been living with the fear of having it stripped away from me, thinking that the way I was doing it was the only way I would be able to keep the weight off. I had brought this scenario on myself to teach me an invaluable lesson.

Minutes after the accident happened, I had identified nutrition as a strong focus I was going to be giving a good piece of my time and attention to. I knew at that point I was going to go deep and develop a plan for myself to move forward no matter what. I restudied several of my favorite nutrition courses, books and programs to compare notes in a contrast study type of format. Yes, I wanted to note all the commonalities within the programs, but my main focus was on the areas of varying opinion. This is where I really dove in and did my research.
This led me to the great T. Colin Campbell, who is a nutrition Yoda for lack of a better description. T. Colin Campbell is the

Jacob Gould Schurman Professor Emeritus of nutritional biochemistry at Cornell University. He was a key partner in the world's largest nutritional study ever, called The China Project, which is documented in his co-authored book *The China Study*. He has written two other books as well as over 300 research papers. He specializes in the effects of nutrition on long-term health. This guy is the absolute real deal.

My studies opened my eyes and empowered me with a new level of certainty in what I was doing and the potential I was creating for myself with the knowledge. Today, I feel more capable than ever in my fit body pursuits because of this experience.

I Fell Off the Wagon

So what happened after a year? What happened is that I got cocky again. I began allowing myself to slip and get sloppy in my consistency with my nutrition. At the time, I couldn't see it, but looking back, when my behaviors and habits changed, it caused a direct effect on every other area of life I was working on. Why? My fit body was slipping and I no longer had the tool I once had to work with. It was taking a serious toll on my progress. Had I stuck 100% to my program, I believe I would have been able to much better in terms of preserving my fit body, but I didn't.

If I would have had a non-biased perspective in order to better coach myself at that time, as soon as I noticed I was slipping I would have gone through the process of asking, "How does recommitting to my fit body goals benefit my highest values?" or, more specifically, "How does recommitting to my fit body goals benefit my family, my finance and business expansion, and my love for nutrition and exercise?" Had I done so, the answers would have been apparent and led me back on target. However, I'm grateful it didn't turn out that way. That may have been just the fuel I needed to remain in that state and I may still be at a place where I am waiting for my wrist to get better so I can start working on the exercise portion of the fit body. This gave me the gift of hitting the bottom and getting off my ass to get my fit body back on track.

Turn Your Frown Upside Down

As we have learned, there is never a negative without a positive. That said, as many of us travel through life, we fail to make this connection when every day we are given the opportunity to do so.

Looking back on the last 24 hours, list something that happened that you feel is a bad thing.

How does this happening benefit what is most important to you in your life, your highest values? More specifically, how does this happening benefit your value #1, value #2 and value #3? (List 25 answers minimum.)

THE FIT BODY

Jim Rohn said, "Staying healthy is the only way to get the good part of all areas of life. It's the way you stay strong and the way you stay interested. It's where the mind and the body meet. It's what the heart, the mind and the muscle are all cooperating for." Jim, you are a bad ass, my friend.

The body is our greatest asset and tool, assisting us to accomplish everything we want in our lives if only we show it the respect and care it deserves. The only way we can do this is to discover exactly what it needs to thrive and give it nothing but that.

A fit life is the end game for all of us. There are seven areas of life and I am willing to bet we all want to thrive in all areas as opposed to just surviving or, even worse, being overcome in these areas. Yes, we can have a fit mind and semi-fit life without including the body, but the end result doesn't compare.

What I find most interesting about the fit body is the fact that the majority of people already know how to get and keep it. Mainly, the fit body is about nutrition and exercise. Most people could tell me exactly what foods are good for you and what foods are not. Also, we all know exercise is a good thing. If this is the case, then why aren't more people practicing these principles? The problem is that most haven't defined their highest values and, therefore, aren't able to see the true value and benefits that nutrition and exercise would be adding to what is most important to them in their lives.

By having a fit mind, we are able to understand the benefits that achieving any goal will have with what we value most in our lives. Adding a fit body to the equation, we put the development of our fit life into hyper drive by enhancing and accelerating everything we are doing down to a cellular level. Without the body in place, everything just moves slower and we are not able to maximize our capacity.

When we reach this point of certainty in our lives, we're able to live life from a different angle. We're not worried as much about what we need for ourselves as our focus moves outwards towards how we can best serve others.

Abraham Maslow developed a theory called "Maslow's hierarchy of needs" in 1943 written in a paper called "The Theory of Human Motivation." Stemming from this, Anthony Robbins created a model, which he calls "The 6 Human Needs." I feel this beautifully explains the concept above.

Tony Robbins has worked with over three million people all over the world and has come to find that people are motivated intrinsically by the fulfillment of six human needs. He says that these are not simply wants or desires but heartfelt and burning internal needs, which link to every decision we make. That said, as I lay these out, you will see a direct overlap between these six core needs and the seven areas of life (spiritual, mental, finance, family, work, social, physical).

Personality Needs:
1. Certainty – *the need for safety, stability and security*
2. Uncertainty – *the need for variety, surprise, challenge, excitement and change*
3. Significance – *the need to have meaning, be special, be needed, be wanted and be important*
4. Love and Connection – *the need for relationships, approval, intimacy and love*

Spiritual Needs:

5. Growth – *the need for constant emotional, intellectual and spiritual development*

6. Contribution – *the need to give beyond ourselves, to care for and serve others*

What most of us chase in our lives is certainty and significance. Why? Because of perceived lack in our lives. These are approval mechanisms. When we don't feel as though our lives are "complete", we search for approval from others as well as things we can depend on to make us feel good. This can be anything from recognition to sex, movies, food, drugs, money, you name it.

If it's something we desire to be labeled as, this is significance. We feel the label helps us define who we are. If it's something we know and know very well, this is certainty. It's comfortable and it's predictable what we'll receive as an end product at all times. We're certain of how we will feel when we watch our favorite movie and eat our favorite foods. What it doesn't do is stretch us.

The more we improve our fit body and wrap our minds around the value it brings into our lives, the more our focus in our lives will move towards uncertainty, growth, contribution, love and connection.

Only when we are comfortable with ourselves first are we able to pursue this fully. When our mind and body are taken care of, it puts us in a position to set ourselves aside and step into the land of uncertainty, contribution and true growth. This allows us to focus on others in terms of how we can contribute to and build new relationships with them. In return, the massive amount of growth we receive ourselves in all other areas of our lives is immeasurable.

"Only those who have learned the power of sincere and selfless contribution experience life's deepest joy: true fulfillment."

Tony Robbins

Setting Your Standards

Whether we call it goal-setting, setting standards or defining our visions, our goals are standards we envision for ourselves, arming us to excel and move forward in our progress in all areas of our lives.

Inherently, as people, all of us share the desire to grow and improve. The hardest fact to face when dealing with this is that failing to set goals and visions in all areas of our lives leaves us disempowered and opens us up to conforming to the values, standards and goals of another person or society as a whole. This can leave us living a life according to the values of others rather than our own. This will be detrimental to maximizing our potential and living a life of true fulfillment.

The solution to this is simple. Know your highest values, set your own goals, and then understand how accomplishing your goals will directly impact your highest values. That's it.

"When your values are clear to you, making decisions becomes easier."

Roy E. Disney

STEP 1 – *Values Hierarchy*

All right, so we are about to jump headfirst into this. At this point, it's important to note that if you intend on taking action with this material, and you haven't yet taken the time to complete the Demartini Values Determination process, now is the time.

Head over to www.drdemartini.com right now and complete the FREE Values Determination process before going any further. When you get to the page, see the menu on the left and click *"Determine Your Values."*

Our values are how we live our lives and knowing these enables us to ultimately know ourselves, love ourselves, and understand exactly why we do what we do and why we want what we want.

Knowing and understanding the impact of values on our lives also unlocks a whole new capacity of how we communicate with others using the platinum rule. Just as it functions with nutrition and the body, the platinum rule works exactly the same with communication between two people.

STEP 2 – *Goals with Deadlines*

Now that we have determined our highest values and can see them in a prioritized hierarchy, it's time to set a new standard for our fit body.

The heart of my *fit mind plus fit body equals fit life* philosophy is that the transformation of the fit mind and fit body together is the greatest catalyst in propelling and accelerating all other areas of our lives. At the same time, it's very easy to set ourselves up for failure here.

Many of us have jumped in and out of fitness and nutrition programs only to find ourselves right back where we started or even worse off at times. When we set goals, they begin as promises to ourselves. If we fail to keep these, what does it say about us? Well, let's say it like it is. It says that we quit.

What happens when we follow through with a goal? We feel amazing. We prove to ourselves that we are capable and, most importantly, our belief and faith in ourselves grow regardless of how big or small the goal was.

How do we ensure that we set ourselves up for success in these situations? We prepare ourselves.

First, we define the goal itself and set a deadline for achieving it. Next, we list how attaining the goal is going to benefit our highest values in our lives. Finally, we reinforce the longevity of maintaining the goal by identifying the drawbacks failing to keep the goal has on our highest values.

Specifically defining both our long-term and short-term goals for the physical area of our lives paints the picture of our own individualized *"fit body."* What exactly is the fit body in your eyes?

When filling in your goals below, consider these additional questions to further your thoughts. What do you want to be with your fit body? What do you want to do with your fit body? What do you want to have with your fit body?
Visualize what you want, and write it down.

Goals with Deadlines	
Define Your Long-Term Fit Body Goal – 1 Year	
Define Your Short-Term Fit Body Goal – 1 Month	

STEP 3 – Your Reasons Why

As people, we never do anything in our lives unless we perceive we will benefit in some way, shape or form from it. This isn't a bad thing or a good thing, just a fact of how we function.

Every day in every way, all decisions we make are processed this way inherently. If we feel doing something will benefit our highest values more than not doing it, we will do it. At the same time, if we feel taking action is a drawback to our highest values, we won't.

Take, for example, volunteer work. We benefit from the situation because it makes us feel ... good. Yes. We are giving back to others without a doubt. At the same time, we get to feel what it's like to contribute and make an impact in someone else's life. Not only an incredible experience for the person receiving but also for the one giving.

Let me ask you... If volunteering made you feel bad, would you do it?

In order for something to be valuable to us and worth our time, we need a clear understanding of the specific value it will be adding or stripping from our lives.

Now, I know on paper this all sounds easy enough, but the fact is that when we face larger challenges in our lives, the process becomes foggy and we lose focus. Why? Because most don't have a clear understanding of their highest values. When we do, we're able to see how our actions directly impact what's most important to us at all times. When we don't, we're unaware of this connection and our reason to follow through becomes non-existent.

This is the challenge with the fit body. If we're not in tune with our highest values, it is impossible for us to understand the value attaining and maintaining the fit body will deliver us.

Let's get serious. Getting a fit body is not easy. If it were, every person would have the body they desired. The fact is that this is far from the truth, especially in the United States. Unless we are able to directly see how accomplishing our fitness goals will benefit our lives, there isn't enough value for us to fully commit to the process.

You already defined your highest values. You also defined your long-term and short-term fit body goals. Now I'm going to bring you through a small series of questions asking how accomplishing your goals will benefit your highest values in your life. When we do this, we see the real reason for reaching our goals. In the end, it has nothing to do with the goal itself. It's all about what will be enabled in our lives once we achieve the goal.

Whether your goal is losing 30 pounds or 200 pounds, only you can decide what will deliver you the true end result you are looking for. The answers you wrote above for your long-term fit body goal and your short-term fit body goals are just that. In our minds, once we get there, whatever we feel is missing will be re-engaged. Guess what? With everything I've observed helping thousands of clients transform over the years, along with my own personal transformation, I feel this is 100% correct. Perception is reality.

Specifically defining the benefits we will be gaining with what is most important to us in our lives builds an immense amount of value. This value creates the ability to accelerate and push through higher-level challenges along the way. Why? Because we see it's worth going through the pain in front of us to get to the pleasure on the other side.

Let's Get Started

Your Reasons Why

NOTE: Expect to have many repeat answers the further you get into the exercise.

Directions
- *As you answer the following six questions, place your pre-defined goals and values in the spaces indicated.*
- *Answer eight to ten benefits for the following six questions.*

EXAMPLE:

How does *(Your LONG-TERM Fit Body Goal)* _____
___*LOSING 65 POUNDS*___ benefit *(Value #1)*
___*MY FAMILY*___ ?

Benefits:

1) I'll be a better dad and husband overall	6) I'll be fulfilled knowing I'm giving my absolute best to my family with my family
2) I become a better example to my family	7) I will have new confidence to better provide for my family
3) I'll have more energy to give my family	8) I'll better be able to provide for my family
4) I'll have more quality focused time to enjoy with my family	9) I'll feel awesome all the time and my mood will reflect that
5) I'll be more present and patient with my family	10) I'll position myself to best take care of my family

Now it's your turn...

1. How does *(Your LONG-TERM Fit Body Goal)* _____
_____ benefit *(Value #1)*
_____*?*

Benefits:

1)	6)
2)	7)
3)	8)
4)	9)
5)	10)

2. How does (*__Your LONG-TERM Fit Body__*
   *__Goal)__*_____ benefit *(__Value #2)__*
   _____**?**

Benefits:

1)	6)
2)	7)
3)	8)
4)	9)
5)	10)

1. How does accomplishing (*__Your LONG-TERM Fit Body__*
   *__Goal)__*_____ benefit *(__Value #3)__*
   _____**?**

Benefits:

1)	6)
2)	7)
3)	8)
4)	9)
5)	10)

2. How does accomplishing (*Your SHORT-TERM Fit Body Goal*)_____ benefit *(Value #1)*
_____?

Benefits:

1)	6)
2)	7)
3)	8)
4)	9)
5)	10)

3. How does accomplishing (*Your SHORT-TERM Fit Body Goal*)_____ benefit *(Value #2)*
_____*?*

Benefits:

1)	6)
2)	7)
3)	8)
4)	9)
5)	10)

4. How does accomplishing (*Your SHORT-TERM Fit Body Goal*)_____ benefit (*Value #3*)_____?

Benefits:

1)	6)
2)	7)
3)	8)
4)	9)
5)	10)

Your Reasons Why: Sum It Up

Directions
- *Answer the last two questions in the most concise way possible.*

---

1. What is accomplishing your goals going to enable in your life?

_____

_____

2. What will be the drawbacks in your life if you give up and don't fulfill your goals?

_____

_____

THE FOUNDATION OF THE FIT BODY

As I'm sure anyone reading this can guess, attaining a fit body consists of a consistent nutrition and exercise regimen. We'll get into more depth about that coming up, but before we do, let's talk about the foundation of the fit body.

The core of the fit body, or maybe more appropriately the foundation of the fit body, is very simple and depends on two variables—a master plan and making the choice to make it happen.

A Master Plan

If you don't have a GPS, roadmap or a compass, you are lost. Your master plan is your GPS. If you have a goal but you don't have a master plan to attain the goal, how will you ever get there?

The truth is that if you are failing to plan, you are planning to fail. Things don't just happen without thought, planning and actions being taken. If we actually want the fit body we say we want, it serves us big time to have a strategy in play to ensure we come out on top through the challenges along the way.

A master plan is not a one and done situation. It requires assessment, changes, refinement, effort and top of mind awareness throughout the journey. Ignoring and neglecting the master plan leads to a decline in progress, just as with anything else we decide to ignore in our lives. On the other hand, creating and following the plan leads to the progress we are looking for.

Setting up your master plan for your fit body is very simple and the great news is that you have already completed step one.

I think it's fair to say that we now live in a world where we all have access to some sort of smart device whether it's a phone, tablet or computer. It's time to use our resources, baby!

Together, we are going to use your phone or tablet to set up a "set it and forget it" reminder schedule that will enable you to keep your plans intact and fully-fledged moving forward if and only if you follow the plan.

Step 1: Set your fit body annual and one-month goals. CHECK!

Step 2: Set your reoccurring annual goal-setting appointment with yourself.

Your annual goal-setting appointment with yourself.
1. *Set a **yearly** repeating appointment using your device, calendar or reminder application.*
2. *Step up and show up to your appointment with yourself.*

Step 3: Set your reoccurring monthly goal-setting appointment with yourself to review the past month's progress and to set your next monthly goal.

Your monthly goal-setting appointment with yourself.
1. *Set a **monthly** repeating appointment using your device, calendar or reminder application.*

2. *Step up and show up to your appointment with yourself.*

Step 4: Set your reoccurring weekly progress appointment with yourself to measure your results for the week.

Your weekly check-in appointment with yourself.
1. *Set a **weekly** repeating appointment using your device, calendar or reminder application.*
2. *Step up and show up to your appointment with yourself.*

Step 5: Surround yourself with your goals and your why daily through anchoring.

Anchoring is a reminder method where you write goals on mini Post-it notes, for instance, and place them in frequently traveled landmarks throughout your life. These are used to keep your goals in your top of mind awareness and keep you focused on exactly what you are out to achieve every time you see them.

To surround yourself with your goals and your why, complete the following exercise.
1. *On eight to ten mini Post-it notes, write...*
   1. *Your one-year fit body goal*
   2. *Your one-month fit body goal*
   3. *Your why*
2. *Place them: In your car, on your desk, on your nightstand, in your living room, or anywhere else you spend your time.*

Making and keeping these yearly, monthly and weekly appointments with yourself displays your commitment to your fit body goals. If you aren't able to commit to these appointments, then you haven't created enough value for yourself to do so.

To give you an endless supply of value and momentum every day throughout your journey, surround yourself with your big-picture goals you're focusing on and your why at all times. It's like hitting the turbo button on a racecar again and again, creating a blanket of continuous inspiration and top of mind awareness of what you want and why you want it everywhere you go. With our goals always in front of us, our actions naturally align and we make shit happen.

Now it's time to take action. Let's set our appointments and create our Post-it anchors from above right now before moving on.

Making the Choice to Make It Happen

You say you want to transform your body and live a certain life, but talk is cheap. Action is everything. "The only truth with our desires and goals is the action we take or do not take to move us closer to or further away from them." This all begins with a choice.

Is this something you really want, desire, love, and are choosing to do? Or is it something you feel you should do, have to do, need to do? In other words, are your goals truly for you or are they what your family or society says they should look like? So maybe I'm a little off with the context of my story, but if the content of what I just said resonates with you, then you know exactly what I'm talking about here.

Who knows? Maybe you aren't even committed to the goal at all. Maybe the goal isn't even yours. Maybe it's what someone else wants for you. Maybe you are just committed to getting the attention you crave, giving you significance. Maybe you fear you will transform and that you still won't be good enough to make the impact you dream of making.

Or maybe you really do want it but you haven't identified enough reasons why. You haven't built the value of what it is going to be adding to what is most important to you in your life, lessening your fear of the situation and making it worth diving headfirst into action.

One of the best quotes I've heard is, "When the why is strong enough, the hows take care of themselves." When we stack our reasons why behind what we desire, there is a breakthrough point where it becomes a must in our lives. This is the most effective strategy I've ever come across to build belief and faith in oneself. We have built the value, which in turn completely changes our value in following through until the end. It proves to us that, in the end, we can do anything if we "set our minds to it".

Regardless of the fears we have with the journey, we are willing to take it on because we've identified the value and worth it adds to who we are and what we desire in our lives. Because of this, the challenges and hard times along the way become worth it to get what we want.

The truth about committing to a goal is that there is never only one journey with one victory or one defeat. There are several journeys every single day. The journeys where we are defeated, we learn to analyze what we will do differently next time and why. This gives us the knowhow of what not to do when we face the same or similar challenges moving forward. As long as you are committed to the journey, when you fail, you get up; you learn, grow and continue moving towards your next failure along the way. Why towards your next failure? Because your next failure is only one step away from the next boundary you break.

When we are victorious, we only gain confirmation on the information we thought to be true. We get a pat on our back by others and ourselves for a job well done. Some decide to celebrate their success by pushing harder. Others develop egos from their success and become complacent.

Why? Because when we are victorious, we don't receive any further feedback for growth. The most valuable tool for our growth is the feedback we receive when we fail. Only then do we discover information that will enable us to explode our growth and overall potential to the next level. When we win, the only feedback we get is to do what we just did again. This stuns many people, leaving them lost.

Now, don't get me wrong; victory is always desired and necessary to propel our next level of inspiration. I love to win at everything I do. At the same time, I will say that the greatest leaps in my own life have directly come from the failures that occurred between the victories. Hence why they are absolutely crucial and must be charged towards.

Once you've made the choice, what matters most is that you start moving forward by doing the work exactly in line with what you say you want. This means making the commitment to falling, learning, getting up again throughout the process, and doing it consistently. This is absolutely crucial for a strong start and even stronger follow-through.

Let's face it; everything we do or do not is based on choice. Many times these are very challenging choices, taking us massively outside of our comfort zone. They seem inconvenient and, from the outside, time and money consuming. If we don't understand how crushing these massive challenges will push our lives to a new level, it's tough to commit every single day because we don't see the value. I totally get it and couldn't agree more. There better be a big payoff or why would we put ourselves in that position? Believe me ... there most certainly is.

Every goal we achieve, every ambition we follow and every challenge we overcome is always a result of a choice we commit to every day of making it happen no matter what. This is what it means to have a fit mind. If your mind doesn't understand the true impact achieving what you say you want has on what is most important to you in your life, it does not understand the value of following through, and how could it quite frankly? Your mind doesn't understand why the pain is worth it for what you receive in return. It doesn't understand that the greater the challenge you crush, the greater the reward you receive in your life. If your mind is not fit, you will give up, you will make excuses, you will procrastinate, and you will not make it to the finish line. Period.

The best example I can think of is for all the parents out there. I think we can all agree that we wouldn't trade our children for anything in the world. At the same time, I think we can also agree that it isn't all sunshine and hundred-dollar bills. There are days of bliss and days we are brought to our personal limits with challenge. For that, I'm eternally grateful because there is no growth in life without challenge. I would never give it up when it came down to it. The pain is worth it for the pleasure I receive in return and that is why I choose it.

For those who have chosen not to have kids, the pain is not worth the pleasure they receive in return according to their personal values structure. Is that a bad thing? Absolutely not. In fact, it's perfect for this person. It's the fulfilled life they had envisioned and have made a reality. In this case, by asking how kids benefit their highest values, yes, the person is able to see the value having children would bring into their lives because they are most certainly there. But, nonetheless, the choice is made that it isn't in alignment with what they desire for their lives.

A fit mind gives us the ability to see the entire picture of all benefits and drawbacks involved in all situations. This gives us clarity of exactly what we desire and enables our decisions, and therefore our actions, to speak from the heart.

This all sounds simple enough on paper, I know. The reality is that in order for any of this to work, it all depends on the choice of one person to apply the work. You.

Every day, all day, we make choices from the moment we choose to get out of bed until the moment we choose to go to bed that night. When we recognize the fact that every action we take causes a reaction in our lives, things get real very quick. Suddenly, we realize that the commitment to transforming our bodies consists of battling temptation and continually deciding if following through is worth it or not in our life.

I know I'm making this sound glorious. This brings us to the logical question: "What's in it for me?"

As people, we never do anything unless we are going to benefit from it. When people say things to me like, "Man that seems like a ton of work. What's in it for me?" my answer is very simple. When you push yourself and transform your body, everything is in it for you in all areas of your life.

You may be stuck in a hole deeper than you think you can shovel out of. So what? People have been deeper than you and literally leaped out. Stop underestimating yourself, get up and fight like it's your life on the line because number 1 it is, and number 2, the life you picture and dream about for yourself is right around the corner ready for you to reach out and grab it.

"Leadership is a choice, not a position."

Stephen Covey

THE THREE IN THREE FIT BODY DAILY PLAN

To make sure we're working towards attaining and keeping our fit body every day, giving it our attention daily becomes crucial.

As you recall from before, when we fail to plan, we are planning to fail. If we fail to have a daily plan, how will we know what specifically to do to move ourselves forward? We are leaving our success to chance and we begin to feel we are losing sight of our goals.

The solution is having a fit body daily plan.

First, purchase a small 5x7 journal you can keep for this and this only. Next, at the end of each day, create your daily plan to set the stage for tomorrow's progress. It only takes three minutes and consists of writing down your plan for tomorrow under three simple yet transformative areas...

1. *Tomorrow's Life Goals*
2. *Tomorrow's Nutrition Goal*
3. *Tomorrow's Exercise Goal*

When we do this, we become inspired. Regardless if we are finishing a very challenging day or an awesome day, this enables us to hold a sense of confidence, excitement and control over where we are going moving forward. We're able to look at the current day and determine what went well and what didn't go well, and, most importantly, write down how we will proceed tomorrow.

By breaking down the fit body into specific daily nutrition and exercise goals, we're able to take a bite-sized-chunk approach to our ultimate goals and literally see our progress continually. When we simultaneously concentrate on our life goals, we become inspired by the fact that not only are we going to be moving closer towards our fit body each day, but we are also going to be advancing everything else we hold dear to us.

I think we can all agree that everyone desires to feel a sense of control over their lives as opposed to feeling out of control. Creating daily S.M.A.R.T. goals not only keeps us feeling in control, they provide tangible steps that if followed will lead us exactly where we want to go. All we have to do is take action and do it.

S.M.A.R.T. goals are Specific, Measurable, Attainable, Realistic, Time-based goals.

Your fit body daily plan enables you to accomplish this format with ease. You are setting specific goals for a 1-day period. Everything is measureable at the end of the day with a simple yes I did it, or no I did not. This makes it very simple to keep your goals realistic, accurate and attainable. The daily plan focuses on continual progress forward with each goal having only a 1-day timeframe to complete it. After that, the clock is reset and you go after it again the next day.

Tomorrow's Goals

Every single person inherently has goals and desires for all areas of their life whether they have clearly defined them or not. Where we tend to invest most of our time and efforts, however, rests with our highest values or what we hold most valuable to us in our lives.

Seeing and, even more importantly, feeling progress in those areas leaves us feeling inspired and empowered in our pursuits. That said, creating S.M.A.R.T. goals every day around our highest values adds a massive amount of fuel to the fire of our actions, attitude and progress every day.

Tomorrow's goals represent one or two goals you want to accomplish tomorrow that will help you fulfill your highest values.

Whether one of your highest values is family and you make a goal of spending an extra hour with them tomorrow or one of your highest values is work and you make a goal of getting up two hours early to give yourself time to crush the project you have been putting off is completely up to you.

Whatever will lift you up and add more inspiration and drive to your progress tomorrow is what you set for tomorrow's goals.

Why only one or two goals? Well, when we have one thing to concentrate on, we are focused. When we have two things to concentrate on, we still may be focused, but our concentration becomes separated. Now picture having four or five different goals you are trying to concentrate on in a 1-day period of time. Suddenly, we find ourselves not accomplishing any of them because we are overwhelmed and don't even know where to start.

Where will that leave us? Feeling like we failed ourselves, which is not the case at all. Truthfully, there is only so much we can do in one day. If we over plan for a 1-day period of time, we are setting ourselves up for failure, which makes this plan a not so S.M.A.R.T. one.

Believe me when I say I am all about setting our standards extremely high. At the same time, when we continually come up short, in a way we become disheartened, frustrated and turned off by the experience. This is exactly the opposite of our objective here.

If you find you reach a point where you are crushing your daily goals and want to add a higher level of attainable challenge for yourself, by all means take it up a notch and add another goal to your list for tomorrow. It must be noted, though, that this must be earned through accomplishment. Once you earn it, set those goals as high as you are able to climb.

Tomorrow's Nutrition Strategy

Tomorrow's nutrition strategy is all about setting the bar a bit higher and becoming a bit more fine-tuned with your nutrition each and every day.

Each night, you will be able to analyze your performance with nutrition by looking at the successes and failures of the day; then choose one new strategy that you will be focusing on the next day that will propel you forward towards your fit body.

Every day through this journey, you will learn more about the process of transformation and, most importantly, about yourself. Some days will be smooth where you just crush it. Other days will not be so smooth. In fact, some days will feel like the most challenging day you have ever had. I say bring those days on because the greater the challenge, the greater the reward. These are the days when we fall and potentially come up short. These same days provide us with an incredible amount of feedback as to how we can move forward differently tomorrow.

Here you are able to ask yourself the crucial questions as you brainstorm what will bring you one step closer to achieving your fit body nutrition. Questions like...

- *What am I going to eat tomorrow?*
- *Who is going to prepare it?*
- *Do I have my protein shakes for on-the-go meals?*
- *Would it be wise to consider delegating my cooking? I just can't seem to get a handle on it.*
- *Do I even enjoy cooking or would I rather have that time for myself?*
- *Why do I always feel hungry? I think I should add more to my portion sizes.*

Tomorrow's nutrition strategy will be whatever you feel will give you the greatest return tomorrow. To give you a couple examples, this can be things like...

- *Tomorrow, I will time my meals because I lost track of time and missed two meals today.*
- *Tomorrow I will drink 12 cups of water instead of eight.*
- *Tomorrow I will prep my meals at night for the next day.*
- *Tomorrow I will go shopping so I have what I need moving forward.*
- *Tomorrow I will contact a food prep company to help prepare my dinner meal for me. Dinners are tripping my progress.*

- *Tomorrow I will adjust my serving sizes because I just wasn't hungry at mealtimes.*
- *Tomorrow I will make my meal three a shake meal because I have a meeting where my meal three takes place.*

Tomorrow's Exercise Strategy

Just like your daily nutrition strategy, tomorrow's exercise strategy is all about continual improvement every single day. The question I have is that if we aren't measuring how we are doing every day, how will we know what to do to get better tomorrow? There is a simple answer here, my friend. We won't.

Each night, you will be reviewing your exercise performance for the day then choosing one new strategy that you will be focusing on the next day that will propel you forward towards your fit body.

One thing to consider with your daily exercise strategy is that there will be scheduled rest days in your week. If this is the case, how are you supposed to set a strategy you will be focusing on for your rest days? I recommend the strategies on your rest days being more directed towards the support side of exercise. Making sure all your workouts are scheduled. Making sure your workout clothes are washed. Doing a foam rolling-and-stretching routine to keep your body extra loose or even taking a walk.

During your evening review of the day, you will be able to ask yourself questions like...
- *Did I exercise today or was it a planned day off?*

- *Was I scheduled to exercise today but missed it?*
- *Am I scheduled for a workout tomorrow? If so, what time? Do I have it in my calendar?*
- *Is my body feeling stronger today than it did yesterday?*
- *Is there anything extra I could have done today to push me forward faster?*

When it comes time to set your exercise strategy you will be focusing on for tomorrow, you will be looking for whatever strategy you feel will give you the greatest amount of return tomorrow. To give you a couple examples, this can be things like…

- *Tomorrow I will work out for three minutes longer than I did my last workout.*
- *Tomorrow I will wake up at 5:30 a.m. so I can get my workout in before work.*
- *Tomorrow is my day off, but I will foam roll and stretch to get my body loose.*
- *Tomorrow I will schedule my workouts for the next month so it is set in stone.*
- *Tomorrow I will use a heavier weight than I did last time when I did my squats.*

I recommend keeping a specific journal by your bed just for this. Each day represents one page in the journal. This will give you an amazing resource to review and reflect on your progress at any time you please.

You may be thinking that this seems like a lot of work. Well, the truth is you are right. In order for accountability to be effective, there is the need for it to be frequent and consistent. Although this may seem daunting and annoying at first glance, what it provides us with is a continual progress and feedback system ensuring we stay close to our target of the fit body at all times. Without it, our goals tend to leave our top of mind awareness and quickly become either forgotten or deemed as unattainable. In other words, we start mind-fucking ourselves right out of our own progress.

Let's get started now!

Your Three In Three Fit Body Daily Plan Format

Date: _____

1. *Review and take notes on your life, nutrition and exercise goals from today using the following questions:*
    a. *What went right?*
        i. _____
        ii. _____
    b. *What went wrong?*
        i. _____
        ii. _____
    c. *What will you do differently next time?*
        i. _____
        ii. _____

2. *Set Tomorrow's Life Goals*
    a. _____
    b. _____
3. *Set Tomorrow's Nutrition Goals*
    a. _____
    b. _____
4. *Set Tomorrow's Exercise Goals*

a. _____

b. _____

So far we have learned a great deal about how to attain the fit body. We learned that in order to have effective goals, they must be S.M.A.R.T. goals. This is why when we set our fit body goals we set "Goals With Deadlines." This consisted of our 1-year goal, as well as our 1-month goal. We also learned to inspect what we expect by setting recurring annual goal-setting, monthly goal review/goal-setting and weekly review appointments with ourselves to make sure we stay on target throughout the process. Finally, we brought it down to the micro level where we just learned about creating our "Three In Three Fit Body Daily Plan."

Now that we have a system in place for setting our fit body goals, it's time to expand our knowledge of the king and queen of everyday strategies you will be using to accomplish your fit body—nutrition and exercise.

"Our goals can only be reached through a vehicle of a plan, in which we must fervently believe, and upon which we must vigorously act.
There is no other route to success."

Pablo Picasso

FIT BODY NUTRITION

When it comes to nutrition, we are what we eat down to a cellular level. Whatever we feed our body is what it uses to feed every single one of our cells. If we feed it what it needs to thrive, it will better serve us in all of our efforts.

In his book, *The Wisdom of the Cells*, Bruce Lipton said, "All cells are the same, but take on a different shape and function as a response depending upon the specific environment they are in." There is not one function in the human body that is not already present in every single cell. For example, you have various systems—digestive, respiratory, excretory, musculoskeletal, endocrine, reproductive, a nervous system and an immune system—and every one of those functions exists in every one of your cells.

I think we can all agree that all cells need fuel. If we decide to fuel them with fast food, milkshakes and candy, what type of environment are we providing for our cellular development and advancement, one that is highly functioning and supportive and that propels us forward or one that challenges our development and holds us back from thriving?

The human organism is very resilient and was created to survive. At the same time, there are optimal fuels that will bring the functionality of every cell in the body to an entirely new level. If we feed the body the foods that will help it thrive, our overall progress will accelerate. If we feed ourselves less than optimal foods, our cells become less efficient and we move into survival mode as they attempt to detoxify themselves and return to a state of equilibrium. Everything just slows down.

Think of it this way. If you feed a racecar regular fuel, it will misfire and not function well. If you feed a racecar its optimal racing fuel, it will devour it and function like a beast!

What I've discovered through all my years of experience is that there is a strong link between optimal nutrition and emotional clarity and focus. Why? Because when you feed your body what is best for it, you feel better physically, you project this energy onto others around you and they feel it. When you don't feel as well physically, that is also projected onto others. In the end, I believe how we feel is how we perform in all areas of life. If we are feeding our bodies optimal nutrition, we will feel unstoppable and perform at a maximal level. If we are not, we become incapable of hitting that level every way you slice it.

"This seems like a lot of effort... How long does this take?"

I'm thrilled you asked.

The beautiful thing is that change in our body begins the instant we change our nutritional habits. As soon as we feed ourselves the wrong foods, the body begins the detox process. As we start fueling ourselves with optimal nutrition, the body uses it to rebuild and repair the damage from our past nutritional habits.

Dr. Jonas Frisen has shown that the body is constantly rebuilding itself. He described the body as being "in a constant state of flux" because of the fact that new cells are continually replacing the old throughout the body. He has discovered that all tissues in the body regenerate at varying rates due to their role and the varying level of demand on them throughout their cell life.

What this means for us is that we have the opportunity beginning now to rebuild our bodies and create an optimal physiological environment, all through what we eat. This is a body environment conducive to thriving and advancing, not a body just hanging on and surviving. Environment is everything in terms of how the cell perceives and responds. The right ecosystem fueled by the right foods promotes an alkaline, relaxed, prepared and focused parasympathetic nervous system environment for all pursuits. The wrong ecosystem fueled by foods that 99% of people already know are not healthy for them promotes the sympathetic nervous system's fight or flight response. Here, your body dives headfirst into detoxification mode, continuously trying to flush and fix the damage caused by our habits and tendencies in a never-ending paralyzing circle.

> *"Let food be thy medicine*
> *and medicine be thy food."*
>
> *Hippocrates*

My Own Journey with Nutrition

From a fit body perspective, nutrition has been my greatest ally with my own body transformation.

My past is that of a binge eater and, over the years, I got myself in a bit of trouble from these habits. Well, when I say a bit of trouble, what I mean is that my life as I wanted it was about 180 degrees away from where I envisioned it being for myself.

Nutrition was not my first step with my own transformation as exercise was. Exercise in itself was beginning to make a real difference for me off the bat. That said, as soon as I found and started vigorously applying my nutrition studies, results began pouring in like never before. It was the marriage between the two that caused the magic to happen.

I instantly fell in love with nutrition because I respected its significance and power in the body transformation equation. I immediately viewed it for exactly what it was. It was a platform to jump to the next level of where I wanted to be.

I became obsessed with it and began researching and devouring everything I could get my hands on from bodybuilding nutrition, athletic nutrition and weight loss nutrition to holistic nutrition and wellness. Next I completed my exercise physiology degree where I more closely studied mainstream nutrition as well as holistic nutrition through the works of Weston Price.

For several years, I applied continuously what I had learned until I was struck with a frightening and also inspiring realization. I knew nothing about nutrition. I was only scraping the surface.

It was frightening because I suddenly realized I had a ton of work to do and so much more to learn. It was inspiring for the exact same reason. I saw the floodgates of limitation with all the questions I still had unanswered.

It was then that I realized that I will never and can never stop learning if I want to be on top of the game. If I am not learning and getting better, I am dying and doing everyone I am striving to service a disservice.

I then began my self-experimentation with everything I could get my hands on in the open mainstream market. I studied everything from the cabbage soup diet and the Atkins diet to the South Beach diet, Paleo, the ketogenic diet, vegetarian, Beach Body nutrition, Weight Watchers, vegan and raw vegan. I became obsessed with learning how to manipulate the body's results through nutrition and exercise.

It was very motivating because I always had something new I was doing, which kept my interests and objectives laser focused, on point and consistent.

The film *Forks Over Knives* was the next turning point for me. This opened my eyes to exactly what I was looking for moving forward—a whole new level of nutrition knowledge. Over the next several weeks, I went through every single nutrition documentary I could find on Netflix. After watching each of them several times and taking a massive amount of notes, I was coming to a whole new understanding again of how much I still wanted to learn.

It was awakening because of the massive amount of cross-over and correlation I was becoming aware of and the incredible number of questions I had developed. It was time to dive in much deeper.

I next tore apart several more advanced nutrition books, including *The 80/10/10 Diet* by Dr. Douglas Graham, delving into the misunderstood power of fruit, and *The China Study* by T. Colin Campbell, which is based on the most comprehensive nutrition study ever conducted. Then I read *Eat To Live* by Dr. Joel Fuhrman, which was an incredible combination of many nutrition platforms brought into one succinct system.

After practicing these principles for roughly nine months, I then enrolled into Cornell's plant-based nutrition certification program under the teachings of T. Colin Campbell himself. This extensive three-course certification was completely eye-opening, helping me tie up all loose ends with literally every question I ever had now answered.

Since becoming a plant-based nutritionist, I have brought my own personal nutrition as well as the nutrition programs I serve my clients with to a completely new atmosphere. How to help people not only get results but to also keep their results has now become clear.

"To learn and not to do is really not to learn. To know and not to do is really not to know." Steven R. Covey, The 7 Habits Of Highly Effective People: Powerful Lessons In Personal Change.

What I Do For My Nutrition

I get asked this question all the time. "What do you do for your nutrition?" I am a plant-based nutrition expert and practitioner. Now, before I go any further, I want to be clear here. The reason I do what I do is because out of every single approach I have ever studied and applied, it is what has delivered the best version of the results I am looking for in my life period. It's what I feel enables me to push the bar higher and do what I want to do every single day. To me, the value of this is crucial. Does this mean that every single person has to do what I do to see drastic improvements? Not at all.

What I have learned is that nutrition is a spectrum of multiple tiers of betterness stemming from the roots of having your entire nutrition comprised of fast food all the way to a raw vegan diet and also covers the multiple levels of progress in between. Every level you step up will yield you next-level results. On the flip side, and I will also say what most people don't want to hear, which is that every step you take down the ladder will yield a loss in higher level results. This is simply the law of cause and effect in motion. The more closely you eat exactly what the body was designed to consume backed by science-based research, the better your body will respond. Nothing more and certainly nothing less.

Another question I get asked all the time is, "What made you start with plant-based nutrition to begin with?" I'd love to say it was an instantaneous spiritual awakening, which in a way it was, but in actuality it came in the form of a challenge.

At this particular time, I was back to strictly proteins and vegetables. My good friend Jeremy then challenged me to a 30-day fruit-based nutrition program where the challenge was to eat as much fruit and greens as I wanted to over the next 30 days and to try to gain body fat.

Now, I don't know about you, but I am not one to look the other way when a challenge is placed in front of me. It was game on. I thought to myself, *If anyone can prove this wrong and beat the system, it's this guy.* I spent the first week packing my face with as much fruit and green vegetables as I could get my hands on and, long story short, I was just overdoing it. I was eating so much that I was uncomfortable just because I was trying to win the challenge.

After that, I settled down to still eating a massive amount of fruit and greens to the point where I was never hungry. In just a few short weeks, I was noticing drastic changes in my body and that wasn't all. I began noticing many differences from the need for less sleep to more streamlined focus.

By the time the 30-day challenge was over, I had already made the decision I was going to continue and I did so for quite some time.

Roughly six months later, I began veering off by adding animal products back into my diet. It didn't take me long to realize this was directly affecting all levels of my performance in all areas of my life very noticeably. As soon as I returned to the strict principles I had had so much success with, everything came back and I felt like a million again.

It was then that this just became personally what I decided to do on a regular basis. Yes, I have made many adjustments over the past several years, but since that moment, I have been strictly plant-based and I've never looked back since.

Of course, there are many arguments out there as to why people may want to consider eating a plant-based diet. Animal cruelty for example, or the fact that the food used to support the US livestock industry is more than enough to instantly solve world hunger as uncovered in the documentary entitled *Cowspiracy*.

Another startling fact from this same documentary is that livestock is actually responsible for 51% of the O-Zone depletion compared to the 11% responsibility for O-Zone depletion the entire transportation industry including trains, planes, boats and automobiles is responsible for. This is due to the methane omissions released by the cows, which are 86 times more damaging than carbon monoxide from vehicles.

Another reason you could say is that livestock is the leading cause of resource consumption and environmental degradation destroying the planet today.

You could even argue that eliminating animal products and following a plant-based nutrition program has been proven to lead to the dissipation and reversal of disease consistently, which I delve into more within the next few chapters.

The list goes on and on.

Why I Personally Do What I Do

It's not primarily about the above for me though. No, you will not see me picketing "Eat chickpeas not chickens" or "Let's save the environment from global warming." These subjects are huge and crucial but, however important, they are not my reason. For me, it's about my ability to control and fine-tune the functioning of my body down to a cellular level to maximize my potential in everything I do in all areas of life. Is that selfish? Sure and I accept that. Although what I choose to call it is focused. I am obsessed with my mission of helping others transform their lives and maximizing my ability to make that happen as efficiently and effectively as I'm capable of.

Mastering and continuing to evolve my application of nutrition has led to more me-time with less food preparation time, more consistent energy, less sleep needed, better body temperature control, better moods, less sickness, better mental clarity, a significant increase with focus and longevity of focus, an increase in efficiency, more alertness, a disappearance of physiological food cravings and, maybe most importantly, an advancement in my perception of myself.

Design, apply, track, quantify, study, refine, and repeat. I've followed this pattern for years as I've adopted and played with well over 100 variations of nutrition programs and have found for certain that there's a direct correlation between nutrition precision with consistency and the continual refinement and growth I achieve in all areas of my life.

I've experimented down to the bite. Physically, there is a difference. Call it what you will, but once you have felt what it's like to have your body firing on all cylinders, anything less is just less.

How does this work considering the center of our existence and purpose is always focused on growth and attaining more in all areas of life? To sum it up, my inspiration continues to grow the deeper down the rabbit hole I go. As I've continued to learn and apply, my results have continued to improve. This lights me on fire and drives me to desire the next level yet.

Michael Jordan said, *"The reason I have been so successful is because I've always expected more of myself than others expect of me."*

I love this quote and I try living by this on the daily. Have I perfected it? Well, far from is the truth. No, I am not without error. I royally mess up daily, which is the same reason I also succeed daily.

The way I look at it is if you are pushing yourself out of your comfort zone at all times and if you are right 45 out of 50 times, you are just further ahead in all regards. Sure, people will argue this, which is everyone's right. At the end of the day, I'm simply here to let you know what has changed my life and continues to work for me every day. If others want to hate and choose not to push themselves, that is their right. I would, however, challenge these same people to question their own personal mission and purpose by asking if they feel they are 100% beyond a doubt maximizing their progress towards their goals. If the answer is yes, all power to them. If they answer truthfully, then I say to them, grab a shovel, step out into the unknown and dig. You never know what you are going to find.

Why I Take It to the Level I Do

From everything I have learned so far in my nutrition studies, the most simplistic way I can sum it up is that there are two types of nutrition being taught today.

1) Mainstream nutrition, which is information that is roughly 10 years behind.

For example, have you ever looked into who is creating the nutrition education platform that is being taught throughout many industries from schools to medicine? When you look closely, you will see Dannon along with other large food corporations.

It makes sense that a food company would expand into nutrition education. Where I become a little bit lost is where all of thae sudden Dannon products fit inside of this nutritional model when we all know very well many of these products are not what most of us would consider "healthy."

Now, of course, I realize every downside also has its upside. Dannon has created many jobs for many families and has also given people the opportunity to learn many basic principles of general nutrition.

I would be lying to you if I said this wasn't serving many people. As I mentioned before, nutrition is based upon multiple tiers of betterness. This begins by eating only fast food and improves every step away from that. Yes, Dannon is making an impact. At the same time, I would also be lying to you if I said this is optimal for human performance.

For example, do you think it would benefit a dairy company for people to fully understand the fact that dairy is far from healthy for people to consume? If that truth came to the forefront, the industry would be finished overnight. We would love to think all companies have only our best interest in mind, but the truth of the matter is that, in many cases, the food industry has their own best interest in mind as well, which includes us consuming their products and helping them expand their business.

Of course, many companies can claim negligence to these opinions that I and many others share, but the fact is that the information is accessible to anyone and everyone interested in looking. In my opinion, when accessible information is not captured and utilized, that is the definition of ignorance. The choice is simply to ignore it.

2) Current nutrition, which is information 10 years ahead of mainstream nutrition.

This is nutrition comprised of many mainstream principles in combination with the most current proven nutrition discoveries.

I will be diving into a couple of these principles and modern myths below.

Long story short, I love the challenge of nutrition. I love mastering the art of creating physical change in the body while at the same time maximizing its functionality. I love the opportunity to learn and connect everything I have previously learned to uncover new answers backed with valid research. This gives me certainty in what I am applying to myself and those I'm here to serve.

Before, we spoke about how we are what we eat down to the level of the cell. Our lives are a direct reflection of this in the way our nutrition enables or disables the direction and speed of our progress.

Nutrition follows the universal law of cause and effect. Whatever quality of foods we put in our bodies, our performance will be of equal quality. In other words, if we fuel with shit, we will feel and perform like shit.

For me personally, the reason I take it to the level I do is because I believe it is all about self-perception. Call it right, call it wrong, call it what you will. The fact remains that when I am not in my peak physical form, I am just less than in my own eyes and therefore less in everyone's eyes.

I have committed to being my best and a huge part of that for me is the way I view myself, which exactly correlates with how I put myself out there. I use nutrition coupled with exercise as my daily rocket fuel. When this is off, I feel a drop in everything. Can't I just shake it off? Sure, but the fact remains my energy is lowered when this happens and I feel the drag physically, mentally, with my family and in all other areas of my life.

The law of attraction is a true force happening all around us and also happening for us. It states that whatever we think about we bring about. Whatever we focus our thoughts and energy on is what we manifest spiritually, mentally, financially, in our family lives, at work, socially and physically. It occurs in all areas of life at all times.

From a cellular level, this is interpreted to whatever electromagnetic frequency you emit or resonate, you will draw in its equivalent. This is also known as the law of resonance. Whatever you focus on will attract energy into your life equal in frequency to those thoughts and beliefs, resulting in what is created in your life. In other words, if you are focusing on feeling sorry for yourself, more instances to feel sorry for yourself will pour into your life. If we are grateful not only for support but for every challenge as an opportunity to grow, we will be given more to be grateful for.

We, along with everything that exists, seen and unseen, consist of a rate of vibration. In other words, what we see in physical life is not solid as it appears to be. It's all a vibrating mass of energy. So when the frequency of our vibration is off even minutely, it impacts everything in our lives due to the ripple effect. One degree either way can change your life. When I feed myself low-quality calories, my personal vibrational frequency changes and immediately begins actually repelling the things I desire to attract into my life. And yes, this is relative. The worse I feed myself, even in a single sitting, the more it will change my vibrational frequency and the more repelling it will be to those I desire to attract.

As I began discussing earlier, the electromagnetic current of the heart can be detected up to three feet from the body in all directions using SQUID-based magnetometers. The SQUID is a superconducting quantum interference device used to measure extremely subtle magnetic fields. As people, we subconsciously pick up these signals through our hearts and are able to immediately form perceptions based on our highest values without even realizing it is occurring. It is only after this has happened that the heart sends a signal to the brain letting it know what we feel about the event or person.

This explains exactly what we experience when we meet someone for the first time and we are either immediately drawn or repelled and can't quite understand why.

Many times it is because either someone has similar or opposite values than we do. But regardless, this situation can be depressed or amplified, lessening or increasing our rate of vibration as well as our level of attraction. This determines what and who we attract into our lives. I believe this all stems from our mind as well as our own self-inflictions of what we feed ourselves as fuel. When we know ourselves and feed ourselves optimally, we will shine. When we don't, we won't.

Before, I mentioned that the law of attraction also happens for us. This is because the law delivers us what we focus on. If we focus on fear and doubt, we receive more fear and doubt. When we focus on more growth, contribution and love, we grow, contribute and love more. The law of attraction is a feedback mechanism constantly allowing us to assess it if we are actually receiving what we desire out of our intentions, thoughts and actions.

"Limits, like fear, are often an illusion."
Michael Jordan

Some of My Most Significant Nutrition Takeaways

I thought it would be helpful if I began winding down the nutrition section by sharing a number of personal takeaways, along with some detail surrounding several frequently reoccurring questions I receive that I feel will help others with their progress.

What about protein? How do you get protein without animal protein?

My answer to that is how much protein do we actually need? Everyone knows we need protein, but the meat and dairy industry has drilled it into us so much through marketing efforts that many believe it is the only thing we need.

The reality behind the glamor is that it's been proven that we as humans only need 5–6% of our total calories from protein in order to replace the proteins we regularly lose and to allow the body to rebuild and repair properly. Past this point, growth will not slow down or speed up.

However, 9–10% of total calories from protein is recommended because any time we cook our food, the added heat denatures the quality of the protein and all other nutrients as well. This increase in percentage makes up for the loss in usable proteins. Any consumption in excess of the 9–10% total calories coming from protein will result in a lack of carbohydrates in the diet to be used as fuel. In turn, the body is put into a situation where it then may need to convert some of the caloric energy consumed as protein into a usable carbohydrate. This becomes inefficient very quickly. The simple answer is to ingest the proper amount of carbohydrates to begin with and the body becomes more efficient and effective in all pursuits.

The typical American diet consists of 20% or more calories coming from animal protein sources. T. Colin Campbell, in his world renowned China Project findings, discovered that 20% animal casein protein ingestion, which makes up 87% of cow's milk, consistently led to exacerbated growth of all cells including muscle cells, cancer cells and the onset of a vast variety of other diseases including heart disease, Alzheimer's and many others. When the subjects were brought down to 5% animal protein consumption, the cancer literally turned off consistently as you can see below.

DIETARY PROTEIN AND EARLY CANCER
(Youngman and Campbell, J. Nutr., 1991, Nutr. Cancer, 1992)

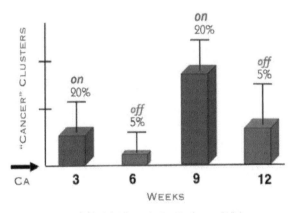

For individual student use only: please do not copy or distribute.
Copyright T. Colin Campbell, 2012

25

Yes, that is correct. A very high level of animal protein consumption has been found to propel cancer and other diseases into rapid growth. In contrast, switching protein consumption to plant-based proteins of the same 20% or under showed no more irregular growth of the cells and no higher levels of cancer development occurred. In fact, the switch turned any further disease development off and actually began to reverse the process just as it did in the diagram above. This unveiled a direct correlation between high levels of animal proteins and the development of disease due to the degradation of the cells.

By the way, in case you are wondering, the level where growth of disease cells took off and began exploding was past 10–12% of calories coming from animal proteins, which you can observe below.

DIETARY PROTEIN AND EARLY CANCER

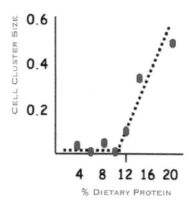

Dunaif and Campbell, 1987

For individual student use only; please do not copy or distribute.
Copyright T. Colin Campbell, 2012

Cavemen ate meat. Isn't that what we are supposed to eat?

We may want to believe we are built to be the carnivore of carnivores, hence the existence of the trendy "Caveman Diet" and many others in practice today. I can certainly appreciate that as I ate meat like a beast for years. Whenever I look at a question like this, I like to look at the studies and the facts we have access to so I can get the greatest understanding of the subject before making a conclusion.

As I studied and studied some more, I came to realize every living organism is built to consume specific foods in order to support its thrival. Yes, most if not all organisms are resilient and are able to survive most things we consume, but that does not mean that we are functioning at our maximum potential. In fact, I can say with certainty that this is a fact.

I'd love to share with you some passages from Dr. Douglas Graham's book *The 80/10/10 Diet* about the differences between humans and carnivores that I found extremely revealing.

- Colon Formation – Our convoluted colons are quite different in design from the smooth colons of carnivorous animals.
- Intestinal Length – Our intestinal tracts measure roughly 12 times the length of our torsos (about 30 feet). This allows for the slow absorption of sugars and other water-borne nutrients from fruit. In contrast, the digestive tract of a carnivore is only three times the length of its torso. This is necessary to avoid rotting or decomposition of flesh inside the animal. The carnivore depends upon highly acidic secretions to facilitate rapid digestion and absorption in its very short tube. Still, the putrefaction of proteins and the rancidity of fats are evident in their feces.

- Microbial Tolerance – Most carnivores can digest microbes that would be deadly for humans, such as those that cause botulism.
- Perspiration – Humans sweat from pores on their entire body. Carnivores sweat from the tongues only.
- Vitamin C – Carnivores manufacture their own vitamin C. For us, vitamin C is an essential nutrient that we must get from our food.
- Jaw Movement – Our ability to grind our food is unique to plant eaters. Meat eaters have no lateral movement in their jaws.
- Dental Formula – Mammalogists use a system called the "dental formula" to describe the arrangement of teeth in each quadrant of the jaws of an animal's mouth. This refers to the number of incisors, canines, and molars in each of the four quadrants. Starting from the center and moving outward, our formula, and that of most anthropoids, is 2/1/5. The dental formula for carnivores is 3/1/5 to 8.
- Saliva and Urine PH – All of the plant-eating creatures (including healthy humans) maintain alkaline saliva and urine most of the time. The saliva and urine of the meat-eating animals, however, is acidic.
- Diet PH – Carnivores thrive on a diet of acid-forming foods, whereas such a diet is deadly to humans, setting the stage for a wide variety of disease states. Our preferred foods are all alkaline-forming.
- Stomach Acid PH – The PH level of the hydrochloric acid that humans produce in their stomachs generally ranges about 3 to 4 or higher but can go as low as 2 (0 = most acidic, 7 = neutral, 14 = most alkaline). The stomach acid of cats and other meat eaters can be

in the 1+ range and usually runs in the 2s. Because the PH scale is logarithmic, this means the stomach acid of a carnivore is at least 10 times stronger than that of a human and can be 100 or even 1,000 times stronger.

- Uricase – True carnivores secrete an enzyme called uricase to metabolize the uric acid in flesh. We secrete none and so must neutralize this strong acid with our alkaline minerals, primarily calcium. The resulting calcium urate crystals are one of the many pathogens of meat eating, in this case, giving rise to or contributing to gout, arthritis, rheumatism, and bursitis.

- Digestive Enzymes – Our digestive enzymes are geared to make for easy fruit digestion. We produce ptyalin—also known as salivary amylase—to initiate the digestion of fruit. Meat-eating animals do not produce any ptyalin and have completely different digestive enzyme ratios.

- Sugar Metabolism – The glucose and fructose in fruits fuel our cells without straining our pancreas (unless we eat a high fat diet). Meat eaters do not handle sugars well. They are prone to diabetes if they eat a diet that is predominated by fruit.

- Cooking and Dry – We are the only "carnivores" that cook our meat and add seasonings to it in order to give it taste. Why? Because it masks what it really is. True carnivores eat the kill fresh, devouring the raw organs and meat, while also lapping up all the blood as well.

Another incredible resource I would love to share is the work of Michael Greger, who is the founder of nutritionfacts.org

and author of the book *How Not To Die*. One incredible passage I want to share with you is directly from his piece entitled "Paleopoo: What We Can
Learn from Fossilized Feces."

"In the U.S., we tend to get less than 20 grams of fiber a day, only about half the minimum recommended intake. But in populations where many of our deadliest diseases are practically unknown, such as rural China and rural Africa, they're eating huge amounts of whole plant foods, up to a 100 grams of fiber a day or more, which is what it's estimated our Paleolithic ancestors were getting based on dietary analyses of modern-day primitive hunter-gatherer tribes and by analyzing coprolites, human fossilized feces. In other words, paleopoo.

These most intimate of ancient human artifacts were often ignored or discarded during many previous archaeological excavations, but careful study of materials painstakingly recovered from human paleofeces says a lot about what ancient human dietary practices were like, given their incredibly high content of fiber, undigested plant remains. Such study strongly suggests that for over 99% of our existence as a distinct species, our gastrointestinal tract has been exposed to the selective pressures exerted by a fiber-filled diet of whole plant foods. So, for millions of years before the first stone tools and evidence of butchering, our ancestors were eating plants. But what kind of plants?

One way you can tell if animals are natural folivores or frugivores is to map the area of absorptive mucosa in their gut versus their functional body size. Folivores are those meant to eat mostly foliage – leaves, while frugivores are better designed to eat fruit. The faunivores, another name for carnivores, eat the fauna.

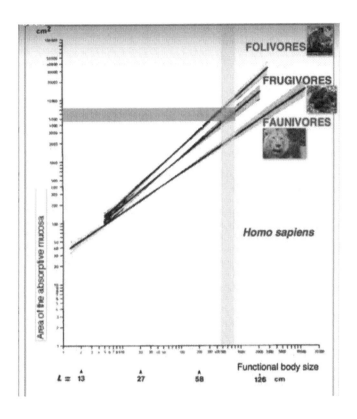

If you chart animals this way, they fall along distinctive lines. So, where do humans land? Here's our functional body size, and here's our absorptive area. So, while eating our greens is important, it appears the natural dietary status of the human species is primarily that of a fruiteater."

When it comes down to it, ask yourself this question. "If there was a pile of your favorite fruit and a live cow in front of you, which one is making your mouth water? Also, which one are you going to walk up to and straight up take a bite of?

What are we meant to eat then?

What I have found through all of my research is that people are best equipped to eat primarily carbohydrates. I believe the ratio of 80/10/10 is very close to exactly what will enable people to thrive. 80% carbs in the form of fruits primarily, green vegetables, and cooked complex carbohydrates such as rice, potatoes, quinoa and beans. 10% protein of which is found inside the fruit, with the remainder being ingested through our complex carbohydrates. 10% fat, which will be ingested through our complex carbohydrates as well as nuts, seeds, and avocado.

The way we eat is a perfect portrayal of cause and effect in motion. When we ingest any food, our body responds instantly in one of two ways. It either accepts what we are feeding it, or it rejects it. Over time, the habits we recycle will determine the long-term outcome of our overall transformation and health in general.

What does it all boil down to?

Everything boils down to the fact that there are two environments we are capable of creating inside of our bodies based on the PH level of the blood. On the one hand, we can create an acidic PH-based fight or flight environment engaging the sympathetic nervous system response. On the other hand, we can also create an alkaline PH-based digest, recovery, rebuild environment activating the parasympathetic nervous system environment. Case in point, animal products along with highly processed foods, including anything pasteurized, create an acidic environment. An acidic environment is equivalent to poison in our bodies. The body goes into fight or flight as it attempts to detoxify itself and return itself to a state of alkaline equilibrium where it can then simply digest, rejuvenate and rebuild. The foods that cause the greatest alkaline response in the human body are fruits and green vegetables.

What about food and disease?

When we speak about the words "body transformation", of course, the first thing that comes to our mind is what we physically look like on the outside. At the same time, I'm sure your true desire for transformation of your body is both outside and inside. This consists of reaching a true level of health and overall wellness, which includes the lack of disease.

The root of all disease is what is called metabolic acidosis. This is a continually high level of acid PH levels in the blood, created through including animal proteins in our nutritional choices. The acids flow in faster than the body can detoxify and the lymphatic system, which is the body's detox system, becomes backed up and overloaded.

There are three phases of disease. Genetically, every single person is different and we all inherit the genes for several different potential diseases. This is considered the initiation phase. We are born with this genetic make-up, but it begins its existence in a dormant state. At this point, we can either keep these potential diseases dormant or aggravate them with our behaviors of what we eat. When we aggravate them, we enter what is called the promotion phase. This is where the disease "turns on" and begins progressing. Once this happens, the floodgates are open and we become more exposed to continued progression of the disease. Continuing the same behaviors that cause the initial aggravation of the cells moves the disease process into what is known as the progression stage. This is where the disease is growing and expanding very rapidly in an out-of-control fashion.

Changing our nutritional behaviors throughout any of these stages has been proven through numerous studies to revert the entire process of disease back to its state of initiation.

CANCER DEVELOPMENT OVER TIME

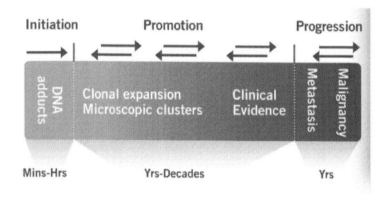

For individual student use only; please do not copy or distribute.
Copyright T. Colin Campbell, 2012

6

CHEMICAL CARCINOGENESIS AND PROTEIN INTAKE AT 12 WEEKS

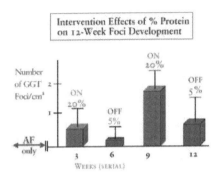

Intervention Effects of % Protein
on 12-Week Foci Development

Experimental tumor development was turned on and off when animals were fed regular levels of protein or much lower levels of protein.

For individual student use only; please do not copy or distribute.
Copyright T. Colin Campbell, 2012

22

So why is it so simple? This is a question I have been asking myself for years. It's because of the fact that we are always trying to over complicate everything, when the truth is that the ultimate in complexity is simplicity.

Carbohydrates are bad right?

I believe this belief is a product of the many mainstream trend nutrition programs floating all over the marketplace.

The fact is that the only fuel every single cell in the body can process as energy is carbohydrates in the form of simple sugars. By the same token, this does not mean processed, refined sugar. This is referring to simple sugars occurring naturally within foods such as fruit sugar. Knowing this, it makes the most sense that if we just consumed the right carbohydrates in the right amounts needed, our body would become more efficient at delivering sugars to the cells for energy. This presumption would be correct, so the only question remaining is why are we depriving ourselves of what we actually need?

We are a processed fast food nation who bases what we eat on taste and speed, not health.

All the while, fruit and vegetables are the least tampered with foods known to man and yet fruits have been labeled as a food "we want to stay away from" because of the fact that it possesses sugar. This is true, but what is misunderstood here is the difference in physiological response when both natural fruit sugar and processed, refined sugars are ingested. The difference is 180 degrees. Fruit sugars help where processed sugar hinders.

What about gluten?

Isn't gluten an inflammatory? Yes, it does have inflammatory principles for sure. What it does not do is aggravate cells into the promotion and progression of disease.

The mainstream nutrition market now is focused on fractionalizing things such as organic, gluten-free, non-GMO and other commonly known pop phrases. What is being missed is the source of the calories. At the end of the day, plant-based foods promote internal health where animal-based foods, especially when consumed at higher levels, cause challenges and degrade our bodies down to a cellular level.

If I eat fruit, it upsets my stomach. Why?

The simple answer is that it isn't the fruit; it's all the other stuff we eat.

The average American eats roughly 33–42% of their calories in the form of fat, and gets 16–25% from protein and the remaining 35–45% from carbohydrates.

If we have a diet heavy in animal proteins, this food is going to take much longer to digest and move through our systems. Throughout this time, the food goes rancid, further upsetting our digestive tract. If we have a diet heavy in animal proteins, this means we also have a diet high in fats, considering the average percentage of fat calories in animal products averages roughly 50–55%. Now, put fruit on top of these habits and we run into a problem. The fruit is sitting in line to be digested because there is a traffic jam waiting to be cleared. Because of this, the fruit becomes slowly digested as opposed to its usual rapid digestion, which causes it to remain in the body longer and begin rotting. This is where the belly begins not to feel so well.

Another thing to add here is that because of the high level of animal protein and fat in the diet, the fat is also dispersed through the bloodstream, not only causing potential long-term health issues but also making it extremely challenging for the sugars from the fruits to be absorbed into the cells quickly and effortlessly as seen in a low-fat diet environment.

Dairy is good for me, right? Milk does a body good, right?

Well … no. That is not correct. Big breath… Here we go.

All dairy including milk and cheese products are actually the most harmful foods we are consuming, the reason being that they contain all three macronutrients of carbohydrates, protein, and fat all in one product. This also means all three of them decompose in their own way. Carbohydrates ferment, proteins putrefy, and fats go rancid. This means all three forms of deterioration are occurring inside of our digestive tract simultaneously. Let's just say the fire alarm is going off inside of our bodies when we eat this. The blood PH levels become acidic and the sympathetic nervous system becomes activated. The body begins its fight or flight response as it attempts to detoxify the blood and return it back to an alkaline PH environment where it can digest, rejuvenate and rebuild.

There is also the myth that we need milk for vitamin D and calcium. First, the vitamin D in milk is not absorbable by the human body. The calcium in milk has also been shown not to be absorbable by the human body. Now, take on top of that the ingestion of dairy produces an acidic response in the body. In order to bring these levels back down, the mineral calcium found in our bones and teeth is needed. This means that it must be leached from our bones and teeth. So the same milk that we are taught is an excellent source of calcium is actually ineffective and, at the same time, taking our internal calcium stores leading to osteoporosis and tooth decay? This is exactly what I am saying.

If you are looking for a great source of calcium, try broccoli. There is as much calcium in one cup of broccoli as there is in one glass of milk, and this calcium actually helps you.

As a side note, the fact that we are the only known species who not only drink milk after infancy but also consume another species' milk is a mystery in itself. The make-up of cows' milk compared to human milk is completely different.

There are different macronutrient proportions along with the hormone structure of another species going into your body.

What happens in the first year of a cow's life? They basically triple in size. Cows' milk is baby cow growth formula. Ingesting this aggravates our bodies down to a cellular level. On top of this, the milk we buy has been pasteurized, more or less severely denaturing all potential nutrients.

Without even considering the industry being known to use antibiotic and growth hormone injections, the fact that we are ingesting another species' hormones in the first place is an extreme no-no. Regardless of the quality of dairy we consume, mixing our hormones with another species' hormones is a recipe for disaster. Animal breast milk is a medium for transporting the hormone IGF-1, better known as insulin-like growth factor, along with hundreds of other chemical components. IGF-1 levels are strongly implicated in prostate cancer, colorectal cancer, premenopausal breast cancer and lung cancer specifically.

Whether you drink regular pasteurized milk, organic pasteurized milk or even raw cows' milk, none of that matters. Ingesting milk or dairy of any kind creates an acidic survival environment more susceptible to the development of disease. The fact still remains: milk is from another species with a completely different nutrient and hormonal make-up. It is made for other cows, not for people.

If this isn't enough, it's also helpful to understand the pus regulations of the dairy industry. Yes, I did say pus. That's right; they allow a certain amount of pus in our milk.

First things first. How does this even happen? With the terrible conditions the animals are housed in, disease and infection run rampant. At any given time, one in 10 cows are suffering from mastitis. During this time, these cows produce an enormously higher level of pus in their milk. Do they stop milking them during this period of time? No, they actually do not. It's business as usual.

The pus regulations for the levels allowed in milk within the United States is one million cells per spoonful. Now, I don't know about you, but I wouldn't want one cell of pus in my family's milk.

The US dairy industry states that the pus isn't harmful because they "cook it" through the pasteurization process. My answer to that is the pasteurization process is not a good thing to begin with. In fact, pasteurization degrades all aspects of food because of the principle that heat destroys. The number of nutrients left after pasteurization is minimal due to many of them being destroyed through the denaturing of the foods. Also, due to the heat involved in the process, coagulation occurs, causing many of the nutrients to mold together into indigestible masses the body then can't get rid of because it doesn't have the proper enzymes to break it down. This then begins to pile up in the lymphatic system.

What is type 2 diabetes?

Type 2 diabetes or "adult onset diabetes" is not a problem with sugar or the body's ability to move the sugar into the cells to then be used as fuel, it is a problem of too much fat in the American diet. Once ingested and digested, this fat runs throughout the entire bloodstream. It coats the inner walls of the arteries and also the receptor sites where sugars are meant to be absorbed and used as energy. It becomes impossible for the body to absorb the sugar we ingest. The sugar just bounces off.

Insulin is released from the pancreas to transport sugar to the cells, but it's ineffective due to the high levels of fat blocking the receptors, so more is released. When this doesn't work, you are now labeled as insulin resistant and diabetic. Take away the high amount of fat in the diet and diabetes goes away. This is something I see in my businesses literally weekly, to be conservative.

Also, regarding all diabetics and fruit, do not be afraid of it. Fruit is the only carbohydrate we ingest that does not require insulin to transfer it to the cell to be used as energy. It is self-serving, meaning it does it by itself and therefore will not hinder blood levels of any who are diabetic. However, if there is a high amount of fat in the diet of the same diabetic, the sugar will be unable to enter the cells due to the fatty sheath blocking it.

DIABETES, FATS AND CARBOHYDRATES

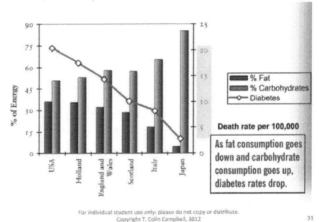

% Fat
% Carbohydrates
Diabetes

Death rate per 100,000

As fat consumption goes down and carbohydrate consumption goes up, diabetes rates drop.

For individual student use only; please do not copy or distribute.
Copyright T. Colin Campbell, 2012

31

So what do you eat?
I wanted to put this in here because I get asked this question all of the time. Grass clippings, dry leaves and

twigs mainly…

In all seriousness, I eat a diet of 78–80% carbs, 10–12% protein, and 8–10% fat.

My main source of carbohydrates comes primarily from fruits, which oftentimes ends up being largely all fruit and greens smoothies. Secondarily, my carbs come from grains like rice and wheat germ, along with quinoa, potatoes and beans.

For protein, the content of protein found in the fruit and complex carbohydrates that I eat is more than sufficient and gets me to and above 10% on the daily.

My fat go-to is avocado for sure. I also eat edamame and occasional nuts and seeds.

Finally, if you are wondering, the answer is yes. I personally am a very boring, mechanical and repetitive eater. Why? Because this is how I love it. I find joy out of finding what is working best through my own experimentation and once I find something that is working well, I repeat it every day moving forward until another tweak comes into play. For me, it is about simplicity and effectiveness. Is this the way I feel everyone should eat? Not at all. Many enjoy cooking and bringing their own creativity to recipes. I think this is awesome and I encourage it.

My Nutrition Coaching Approach

What I believe is it's all about is meeting others exactly where they are. It's not about changing people. It's about living by example in order to attract others to what you do and then gaining an understanding of what they are looking for and why.

Two of the greatest lessons I have ever learned, and also two of the most obvious if we are genuinely focused on helping others, are as follows:

1.) People want to be loved and appreciated for exactly who they are.

Would I be right in saying that you would prefer not to be judged? Same here. Like I said, this seems very obvious, but the question I was asking myself was, "Am I doing this?"

Every single person has a different values structure. What is important to one person is not important to another. So who is right? Both of them. Every person's values are equally important. The only reason we tend to side more with some and not others is because we share similar values.

If we are truly loving and appreciating others for exactly who they are, this means meeting others exactly where they are at without judgment.

2.) Perception is reality. What a person thinks and feels is their reality.

For me, it's about helping others break the same boundaries I have been able to break through in my life. If it's all about helping others, where does being right fit into the equation? The simple answer is that it doesn't. If we are out to help others, then we do what we need to do to help others, period. We drop the ego and begin concentrating on what others need so that we can genuinely help them get what they are looking for.

Every person has their own perspective and opinions stemming from their highest values. If we don't respect this in others, then the question is are we really there to help them or just win the argument of who is right and wrong? If that's the case, then who wins? The answer is no one. The potential client walks away with the same problem they walked in with, and you are unable to help that person.

Like we spoke about before, accepting another's perception is the perfect example of the platinum rule in action. This is the only authentic way to treat others as they want to be treated. To accept is to express love.

Throughout my own personal development, I have learned to never criticize or try to force change with nutrition and exercise on anyone. However, if someone asks me my opinion, I ask them if they want the sugar-coated version or the real version that will actually help them. Then I give it to them. Putting it this way prepares people for the truth, which is generally almost 180 degrees away from what most are currently practicing and from what they want to hear.

I am committed to teaching and putting people in a position to make their own choice. I've learned that trying to convince others to do business with me is not a good situation. It's all about the amount of value we are able to provide and the trust we are able to build with others that make people believe in and want our services. If we aren't providing that and are trying to make a quick conversion, then, in my eyes, we are doing a disservice to them and don't deserve their business.

My personal goal is to provide service that is useful, effective, consistent, simple and approachable. I wasn't always delivering this, however. In fact, looking back several years, I think it's safe to say that, to many, I was unapproachable.

I remember finding myself criticizing what others were doing because it was different than what I was doing and what I thought was right. I found myself hitting a stumbling block where I only wanted to teach what I was doing because I was convinced it was the best and only approach. I thought anything other than what I was doing was just incorrect. I was wrong.

This is when I made the connection of progression to nutrition and came to understand what I referred to before as the multiple tiers of betterness with nutrition. Any improvement is simply that: improvement.

The truth is that most people do not enjoy change and would love to continue exactly what they are doing while also getting the results they want. The key for me is finding that happy medium and making sure to have something to provide people regardless of where they are looking to start.

What I have found is that we as people are always looking for more. When we reach a certain destination, we always want to know what's next. This is where I have found my clients are much more open to the next step and this is when I present it to them. If I tried forcing this and only this on them from day one, I wouldn't have been able to help that person. Even just thinking about that destroys me as this is my personal mission.

"Tough love and brutal truth from strangers are far more valuable than Band-Aids and half-truths from invested friends, who don't want to see you suffer any more than you have."

Shannon L. Alder

I'm Not Ready to Give up My Meat

I completely understand. I have been there. There are many people not even close to ready to give up animal products and that is completely fine.

If that is the case for you, but you still want to improve your health and begin transforming your body and your life, there are many solutions that will help you improve and move forward beyond a doubt.

What I suggest as the best possible version of this would be consuming fish as the primary source of animal products in the diet. That said, fish still wants to be limited and not overdone.

Aside from the fact that too much fish equals too much animal protein for optimal health in general, too much will also expose us to high levels of mercury in the blood, which promotes lipid per oxidation. This is inflammation in the body that causes what are called free radicals. These play a major role in the development of diseases such as heart disease, diabetes and arthritis.

The fish with the highest mercury levels, and the ones we should stay away from, are tilefish, swordfish, mackerel, shark, white snapper and tuna. The fish with the lowest mercury levels are salmon, flounder, sole, tilapia and trout. Eating fatty fish with omega 3 fatty acids has been shown to help prevent blood clotting, reduce the risk of heart attacks and protect the arterial walls from the damage of other fats like saturated fats and trans fats. These fatty fish include salmon, trout and halibut.

There are, however, negatives associated with fish that I must bring to your attention. Higher levels of mercury consumption in mothers has been associated with birth defects in newborn children as scientists believe fetuses are more sensitive to mercury exposure than adults. Researchers are also concerned about other chemicals in fish, including PCBs, which have been linked to brain damage. If fish is consumed in high amounts, it may also interfere with our immune system. High consumption of fish has been found to correlate with lower immune system functionality, leaving us with a lowered defense against cancer and other diseases in general.

Bottom line is that if you are going to eat animal products, choose fish, but the place it was caught and the type of fish matters. Even though we hear fresh caught fish is better, the reality is we have no idea where they were caught. Farm fish is safer. Finally, stay away from high mercury content fish. Optimally, try not eating fish more than two or three times per week.

If eating meat and animal products is a must for you, I feel the model Joel Fuhrman lays out in his book *Eat To Live* does a great job and is backed by sound research science.

The following are some of the principles of the program.

1.) Dr. Fuhrman's Health Equation – H = N/C.

Health equals nutrients divided by calories. This represents eating nutrient dense foods with high amounts of vitamins, minerals fiber and phytochemicals. Next, we want to make sure we are eating choices that are also low in calories. The perfect primary options here are fruits and vegetables. Your primary goal is to eat foods that have a high proportion of nutrients to calories, hence the formula, health equals nutrients over calories.

2.) The 90% rule. Treat animal products as a condiment, constituting no more than 10% of your total calorie intake throughout the week.

He recommends the average woman to eat roughly 1,400 calories per day and the average man to eat roughly 2,300 calories per day. This mean 140 calories for woman and 230 calories for men per day would be from animal products and still fall under this rule. With the 90% rule, many people decide to have days when they don't have any animal products to make sure they are able to stay at or below that 10% total for the week.

Why is this an acceptable level when animal products are linked to the development of cancers and other diseases? In

The China Project by Dr. T Colin Campbell, the findings with cancer and rampant disease development were shown to occur beginning above 10% of calories in the form of animal protein, as seen in the picture below. Above 10% has been shown to send genetic predisposed disease cells currently in the initiation (dormant) stage of development into growth promotion and further progression. This program fits into these principles and is actually based off of them.

DIETARY PROTEIN AND EARLY CANCER

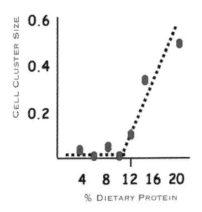

Dunaif and Campbell, 1987

For individual student use only; please do not copy or distribute.
Copyright T. Colin Campbell, 2012

3.) The Life Plan: Dr. Fuhrman's Food Pyramid. I feel this beautifully outlines the categories and proportions of recommended foods to be consumed each day.

Dr. Fuhrman
Guiding You to Great Health

NUTRITARIAN FOOD PYRAMID

- BEEF, SWEETS, CHEESE & PROCESSED FOODS — RARELY
- POULTRY, OIL EGGS, FISH & FAT-FREE DAIRY — LESS THAN 10%
- WHOLE GRAINS & POTATOES — 20% OR LESS
- SEEDS, NUTS & AVOCADOS — 10-40%
- FRUITS — 10-40%
- BEANS LEGUMES — 10-40%
- VEGETABLES* 1/2 RAW & 1/2 COOKED — 30-60%

TOP 30 super foods

NUTRIENT SCORE

#	Food	Score	#	Food	Score
1.	Kale, Watercress	1000+	16.	Artichokes	244
2.	Collard, Mustard & Turnip Greens	1000+	17.	Strawberries	212
			18.	Pomegranate Juice	193
3.	Bok Choy	824	19.	Tomatoes	190
4.	Spinach	739	20.	Blackberries	178
5.	Brussels Sprouts	672	21.	Plums	157
6.	Swiss chard	670	22.	Raspberries	145
7.	Arugula	559	23.	Mushrooms	135
8.	Radish	554	24.	Blueberries	130
9.	Cabbage	481	25.	Papaya	118
10.	Bean Sprouts	444	26.	Oranges	109
11.	Romaine	389	27.	Beans (all varieties)	57-104
12.	Broccoli	376	28.	Seeds - Flax, Sunflower, Sesame	52-78
13.	Red Pepper	366	29.	Onions	50
14.	Carrots	336	30.	Walnuts	34
15.	Cauliflower	295			

The Six Habits of Highly Effective Weight Loss With Any Nutrition Program

Habit 1: Eat six equally sized meals per day. DO NOT SKIP MEALS.

Habit 2: Eat every 2.5 hours and adjust serving sizes if too much or too little food. If you are full at 2.5 hours, drop the portion of each component until you find the correct amount getting you to 2.5 hours where you are ready for your next meal. If you are hungry before 2.5 hours and the meal has fruit, add more fruit. If hungry and the meal does not have fruit, increase all components equally.

Habit 3: Anytime you are hungry outside of mealtimes, eat fruit, but eventually adjust that meal by increasing portions to get you to the 2.5-hour mark.

Habit 4: Drink half of your bodyweight in ounces of water per day minimum with the goal of 1 gallon. No chemically altered drinks such as soda, diet soda, beer, milk, etc.

Habit 5: Substitute meal replacement shakes with fruit and greens mixed in for meals where "time" is a factor for you throughout your day.

Habit 6: Be consistent. Any program will only be as effective as it is applied. The closer and longer we follow any program, the better and faster the results will happen.

FIT MIND + FIT BODY = FIT LIFE NUTRITION PROGRAMS

In my mind, this book would not be complete without giving you a plan of action for those who are ready to get moving forward right away.

Below you will find two simple fit mind + fit body = fit life quick start nutrition programs. One program includes animal products and the other is a full plant-based program. These are by no means your perfect, complete solution but meant more as a simple guide enabling you to get started as soon as you desire, without having to wait.

Quick Start Nutrition Programs

FM + FB = FL Quick Start Nutrition Program

Food Choices: Every food item counts as 1 serving

Fruits	Vegetables	Complex Carbs	Proteins
• 1 Medium apple • 1 Cup any berries • 1 Cup any melon • 1 Medium banana • 1 Cup pineapple • 1 Orange • 1 Cup Fruit Smoothie	• 1 Cup steam broccoli • 1 Cup steam spinach • 1 cup steam asparagus • 1 Cup steam cauliflower • 1 Salad	• ¾-1 Cup cooked oatmeal • 4oz Cooked potato – any • ¾ - 1 Cup cooked lentils or beans - any • ¾-1 Cup cooked – any but white	• 4 Egg whites • 3 Ounces chicken • 3 Ounces white fish • 1-2 Scoops Vegan or Whey protein

* Eat every 2.5 hours
* Use the above chart to choose your foods

MEAL 1
> 3-5 Servings Of Fruit
> 1 Serving Of Vegetables

Time:_____

MEAL 2
> 1 Serving Of Protein
> 1 Serving Of Vegetables

Time:_____

MEAL 3
> 2-4 Servings Of Fruit
> 1 Serving Of Complex Carbs

Time:_____

Protein Shake Meal 4
> 1-2 Scoops Of Vegan or Whey Protein
> 2-3 Servings Of Fruit

Time:_____

MEAL 5
> 2-4 Servings Of Fruit
> 1 Serving Of Complex Carbs

Time:_____

MEAL 6
> 3-5 Servings Of Fruit
> 1 Serving Of Vegetables

Time:_____

FM + FB = FL Quick Start PLANT BASED Nutrition Program

Food Choices: Every food item counts as 1 serving

Fruits	Vegetables	Complex Carbs
• 1 Medium apple	• 1 Cup steam broccoli	• ¾-1 Cup cooked oatmeal
• 1 Cup any berries	• 1 Cup steam spinach	• 4oz Cooked potato – any
• 1 Cup any melon	• 1 cup steam asparagus	• ¾ - 1 Cup cooked lentils or
• 1 Medium banana	• 1 Cup steam cauliflower	beans – any
• 1 Cup pineapple	• 1 Salad	• ¾-1 Cup cooked – any but
• 1 Orange		white
• 1 Cup Fruit Smoothie		• ¾-1 Cup cooked quinoa

* Eat every 2.5 hours
* Use the above chart to choose your foods

MEAL 1
> 1-2 Serving Of Fruit
> 1 Serving Of Complex Carbs
> 1 Serving Of Vegetables

Time:_____

MEAL 2
> 3-5 Servings Of Fruit
> 1 Serving Of Vegetables

Time:_____

MEAL 3
> 1-2 Serving Of Fruit
> 1 Serving Of Complex Carbs
> 1 Serving Of Vegetables

Time:_____

Protein Shake Meal 4
> 1-2 Scoops Of Vegan Protein
> 2 Servings Of Fruit

Time:_____

MEAL 5
> 1-2 Serving Of Fruit
> 1 Serving Of Complex Carbs
> 1 Serving Of Vegetables

Time:_____

MEAL 6
> 3-5 Servings Of Fruit
> 1 Serving Of Vegetables

Time:_____

FIT BODY EXERCISE

Nutrition is king and exercise is queen. Yes, it is true that you can never out-train a poor diet. That said, the significance and the results of exercise are outstanding, especially when they join forces with a solid nutrition program.

Exercise is very simple for all of us really and Nike says it best. Just Do It. Period. Of course, there are excuses from time to money. My answer to that is exercise buys me time and makes me more money. I need less sleep, which makes up for the time, and I feel more vibrant and capable in everything I do, which has driven a whole new level with my businesses. And that's just the tip of the iceberg. What lies beneath the surface is the growth and transformation in my own personal belief and faith in myself. This is literally gasoline on the fire every single day for me and so many others.

So what do I do, how often, how much and when? I understand. We have traveled through a tremendous amount of information here together. I want to break it down for you in a model you may be familiar with. It is the FITT model. FITT stands for frequency, intensity, time, type.

Frequency is how often someone wants to be training their body. The true answer here is that it depends on the goals that you have. As a rule, whatever you put into it is what you get out of it. If you exercise more frequently, exert maximum effort when you do, and are more consistent with your routine, you will achieve better and faster results than someone who does not.

If you are looking to lose weight and achieve a lean, sculpted look, I recommend four days of strength training per week. Two days of light to medium impact physical activity and stretching every day.

Movement in my opinion is essential every single day. Whether you are scheduled to go to the gym or not, stretching every day is tremendously beneficial to all of us. Simply put, stretching and full range of motion movement increase flexibility and flexibility is the fountain of youth. Over time, through disuse due to a lack of physical activity, the body begins to lock up and the muscles begin losing elasticity. This can begin to reverse instantly with a consistent regimen.

Intensity How hard do I need to push myself? Ironically, "How hard do I want to be pushing myself to get the results I desire" is a question I very rarely if ever hear when, in fact, knowing this is a necessity in the exercise formula.

Yes, the concept of exercise is very easy. It's just a matter of getting off our asses and doing it. That said, if we are just going through the motions and not putting our bodies in challenging and uncomfortable situations, why the hell would we ever advance or improve?

It comes down to the fact that if you really want to transform your body, it's necessary that you push your body past the point it's currently comfortable with and capable of. If we fail to do this, we aren't giving it a reason to improve because it can already do what we are asking of it. It really is that simple.

Time When is the best time to exercise and how much time should I allow it for? Whenever I am asked this question, I always answer whatever time you won't have the opportunity to make excuses about not doing it.

For me, personally, I find that first thing in the morning before anyone else is up is the best time. In this case, if it doesn't happen, there are no excuses. The only person who got in my way that day was myself. Regardless, whatever time you choose must be a non-negotiable time. This is you-time.

As far as the amount of time you spend exercising. Aside from an 8–10-minute warm-up, 30 minutes of high intensity performance training is plenty to achieve a fit body. However, I strongly recommend not exceeding 45 minutes of HIPT. Past this point, the body begins to fatigue fast and form begins to unconsciously degrade as the body attempts to compensate for the movements it cannot perform well any longer.

Type Of course, my opinion here may be a bit biased, but through my 22 years of research and application, if your goal is weight loss and body transformation, I believe the best approach is high intensity performance training. If you are looking to become a bodybuilder or a professional sprinter, this is not the best approach. Like we mentioned before, different goals require a different approach.

At my company, Core Capacity Transformations, our full body formula is designed for maximum weight loss and body transformation in the least amount of time. What we specialize in is helping people lose the weight and keep it off for good.

We have split the body up into push and pull segments in order to work your push muscles today and then work your pull muscles tomorrow while your push muscles rest. This way you have automatic built-in rest for the muscles you worked the day before and prevent overtraining and potential injuries.

With our push and pull design, we are able to work all areas of the body for maximum muscle engagement, which is essential for fat burning and weight loss. The key is that while one muscle is working, its antagonist muscle is resting. For example, while the chest is working today, the back is resting. While the triceps are working, the biceps are resting. While the front of the legs or quadriceps are working, the back of the legs or hamstrings are resting. This way we are still working the lower body, the upper body and the arms, while also resting the muscles of the lower body, upper body and arms at the same time.

A question I also receive a lot is "Is it a good idea to work legs every day?" The answer to this is yes if you do it correctly. First things first, engaging the lower body in exercise releases the greatest amount of testosterone, further enabling the rest of the body to produce and maintain fat-burning muscle. If you do the same exercises every single day, you will not get the end result you are looking for. With the push and pull split I explained above, you are able to work your legs literally every day by basically training half of the leg one day and the other half the next day. There are plenty of exercises to keep this very interesting and plenty challenging. In my opinion, this frequent engagement is necessary to maximize anybody transformation.

HIPT High intensity performance training in a heart rate (HR) controlled environment. The difference between traditional HIIT or high intensity interval training and HIPT is that high intensity performance training not only concentrates on strength gain in a fluctuating heart rate environment, it also focuses on functional everyday human performance development.

In my opinion, there are many training programs out there. What I see lacking is the need for a higher level of intelligence built into the program based on injury prevention and the quantitative assessment of progressive results. Only when we have this information can we make adjustments if needed based on what is going to bring the most efficient and effective result based on the client's goals. For example, our Core Heart Rate training system teaches you how much time you want to optimally spend in each HR zone for maximal weight loss and muscle retention. This is what we call The Core Burn Effect.

What's Your Plan?

Remember, if we are failing to plan, we are planning to fail. We want to be moving every day. I recommend an exercise regimen of the following:

- 4 strength workouts per week on 2 days on, 1 day off, 2 days on 2 days off rotation.
- I recommend filling 2 other non-strength workout days with some type of physical activity that you enjoy like a bike ride, jogging, playing basketball or anything like this. This will keep your body fully engaged with your entire system functioning at top speed at all times.

- Finally, I recommend stretching and foam rolling every day of the week, as flexibility is youth.

The body was made to move and be active. Activity accelerates the performance of the lymphatic system. The lymphatic system is responsible for flushing and draining toxins, waste, excess fluids and infections from all tissues of the body when the system is functioning properly. When it's not, your cells are not maximized, period. In fact, it is quite the opposite. Your body activates the sympathetic nervous system and goes into fight or flight, concentrating on ridding itself of the harmful materials inside of the cells, which it recognizes are not being excreted from the body. It becomes distracted with backlogged work and is unable to recover and improve itself, which can only happen in a parasympathetic rest and recovery nervous system state. Challenging our bodies with strength and metabolism-boosting exercise refreshes and strengthens the lymphatic system, helping it flush waste from every one of our cells.

From everything I've learned I can summarize it like this. The root of all disease begins with acidosis, which is the build-up of lactic acid in the blood stemming from foods that don't agree with our physiology. These acids pour into our lymphatic system in order for us to get rid of them. The problem is that, over time, the system gets backed up to where there is more lactic acid coming into the lymphatic system than we can get rid of. Disease eventually moves into what is called promotion, which is where the negative effects begin to accumulate and worsen. Finally, it moves into progression, where the negative effects of the disease speed up even more. All of this is literally caused by the repetition of poor nutrition behaviors over time. This causes more and more waste build-up inside of the internal organs to the point where the waste thickens and it becomes more difficult for the lymphatic system to clear from the body. The toxic byproducts of viruses, bacteria and parasites, which are meant to be excreted, now remain inside of us, leading to the perpetuation and development of disease.

When the contaminated fluids enter the bloodstream, as is part of the normal process, infection can now spread to any organ or part of the body due to the high levels of harmful waste moving through our bodies. Not a place I'm guessing any of us want to be.

The takeaway is that exercise accelerates everything to do with these processes. If your lymphatic system is backed up, exercise speeds up the process of detoxification and excretion of these acids in the body.

"If we could give every individual the right amount of nourishment and exercise, not too little and not too much, we would have found the safest way to health."

Hippocrates

THE SEVEN HABITS OF HIGHLY EFFECTIVE BODY TRANSFORMATION

Habit 1: Warm-up

Never start your body cold. This is exactly like starting your car in the dead of a blistering cold winter and flooring it right away. To properly prepare your body for exercise, we must heat the muscles as well as bring more lubrication to the joints. This can be done through low-impact movements such as body weight squats, jogging in place, jumping jacks, mountain climbers, foam rolling and stretching.

Habit 2: Vary Your Training

The body is extremely intelligent. It adapts itself to new environments and challenges very quickly. With exercise, confusing the body is the goal. This is known as muscle confusion and leads to continual change in the body without plateaus caused by doing the same thing over and over again.

You can create this variety and confusion by changing the format of your workout, changing the order you perform exercises, performing different exercises, changing your repetition scheme and many other variables. The key to remember is that simple changes to vary up your workout routines go a long way with keeping your body always guessing and engaged.

Habit 3: Do It Correctly

Pertaining to exercise, form is king. Form prevents injury and ensures full range of motion along with balanced muscular development. If form is off, all of this goes out the window. Remember, if you get hurt, what good is that to your goals? This is why I always recommend professional guidance from a trainer certified through a nationally accredited organization like ACSM for people of all fitness levels.

Habit 4: Push Yourself
If we aren't pushing ourselves beyond where our bodies are used to being pushed, our bodies will not change and transform. It will say, "Okay, great, I can already do this so I am good." It grows complacent unless we force it into the discomforts of greater levels of challenge.

Habit 5: Flexibility
Full body range of motion is desired by all and truly is the fountain of youth. Lack of movement and ability to move is associated with the aging process. It doesn't have to be this way, however. Yes, of course, with age, the body develops challenges, yet it doesn't have to be as drastic and happen as quickly as it does in our culture.

Your muscle system is what controls your bone movement.
If you are restricted, it's because your muscle is locked up.
To lay it out simply, if we don't use it, we lose it.

Habit 6: Be Consistent
Everyone has worked out and ate healthy for a day. Many people have worked out and ate healthy for a week. Several people have worked out and ate healthy for a month. Few people have worked out and ate healthy for six months, and only the select few people have worked out and ate healthy for a year or longer. It is the select few who are a testament to consistency leading to desired results.

Not only this, but through all of my experience, many people believe they can change all of their nutrition and exercise habits for the better, achieve an amazing body transformation, then revert back to what they were doing before and keep the body transformation. This is what Albert Einstein called "The Definition of Insanity." Doing the same thing over again and expecting a different result. I personally am a testament to that.

Habit 7: Exercise in Under 1 Hour

In order for an exercise regimen to be successful, it must be doable not only from a physical standpoint but also with time. If it was required that we worked out for five hours per day to be in great shape, I would say only a fraction of people doing it currently would continue. The truth is that unless you are an Olympic athlete and training is your job, this is not necessary whatsoever to transform your body. It has to fit into our lives in order to eliminate excuses.

Four strength workouts per week of 30–45 minutes, along with added leisure physical activity and stretching, are plenty to achieve the fit body of your dreams. Past this point, we begin to breach exhaustion where form begins to deteriorate, which leads to injury.

FIT MIND + FIT BODY = FIT LIFE WORKOUT PROGRAM

With the program I created for you below, the design model I used was the push and pull model. Here, one day is all push exercises followed by the next day being all pull exercises. The idea behind this is that while the push muscles in our body are working, the pull muscles are resting. While the pull muscles are working, the push muscles are resting. In addition, I also separated the push and pull into upper body push, lower body push, upper body pull, lower body pull movements to make sure you have a thorough program. Each day will also have core exercises built into the routine, as the core is essential for maintaining a strong skeletal structure.

I have combined all of these elements together into two push and two pull workouts for you that will keep it fresh for you without having to be outfitted with an entire gym in your home with access to hundreds of exercises. In fact, you will only need two pairs of dumbbells.

With any training regimen, changing things around in your workouts frequently causes what is called muscle confusion. This always keeps the body guessing and continuously requires it to adjust and acclimate itself to the new conditions. In other words, the body never gets used to it. The misperception with this is that it takes a massive amount of variety to achieve this. With all of my research and application, I have found this to be untrue. Simply by changing up any or all of the following creates the confusion needed to continually progress.

1. The exercises themselves
2. The order of the exercises
3. Resistance
4. The number of repetitions you use per set
5. The format of your routines

My goal here is to create for you an easy-to-understand, extremely effective program that gives enough variety to challenge the body but is still very simple. The best part is that you can start right away with only two pairs of dumbbells. Enjoy.

Quick Start Workout Program

Below you will find a fit mind + fit body = fit life quick start workout program. Like I mentioned in the nutrition section, this is by no means the best workout program in the world. I created this as a mid-entry-level workout program for people at all fitness levels. This will give you instant access to begin transforming your fit body as quickly as you want to get started with minimal equipment and without having to wait another moment.

* I always recommend consulting your physician for a physical before beginning any exercise regime including this one.

*fit*MIND + *fit*BODY = *fit*LIFE
Quick Start Workout Program

Equipment Needed

2 Sets of dumbbells
- Women recommended weights
  1) 10 lb. dumbbells
  2) 20 lb. dumbbells
- Men recommended weights
  1) 15 lb. dumbbells
  2) 25 lb. dumbbells

* Keep in mind that more or less weight may be needed pending on strength levels. This however is a solid platform to get started.

Repetitions & Sets Explained

REPETITION (REP)

A repetition is doing a movement 1 time. 1 pushup equals 1 repetition.

SET

A set is a group of consecutive repetitions. 1 group of 10 consecutive repetitions equals 1 set.

7 Day Repeating Weekly Workout Schedule

DAY 1	DAY 2	DAY 3	DAY 4	DAY 5	DAY 6	DAY 7
Activity						
Push Strength	Pull Strength	OFF / Stretch	Push Strength	Pull Strength	Physical Leisure / Stretch	Physical Leisure Stretch
TIME SEQUENCE						
30 Minutes	(2) 15-Min. Segments		(2) 15-Min. Segments	30 Minutes		
REPEAT						

Daily Strength Warm-Up

* Set a timer for 8 minutes and repeat the following movements in order for as many rounds as possible.

1) 15 Jumping Jacks
2) 20 Mountain Climbers
3) 10 Body Weight Squats
4) 10 Arm Circles (each)
5) 40-Step Jog In Place
6) REPEAT

4 Strength Workouts **Explained**

1. PUSH STRENGTH 30 MINUTE

The concentration of todays strength workout will be pushing exercises. We will complete a 5 exercise rotation as many rounds as we can complete in 30 minutes.

    a. Reps for each exercise: 9

    b. Exercises:

PUSHUP

GOBLET SQUAT

BENCH TRICEP DIP

WALL SIT

FRONT PILLAR

---

2. PULL STRENGTH (2) 15-MINUTE SEGMENTS

The concentration today's strength workout will be pulling exercises. Your goal is to complete as many rounds of the exercises in segment 1 as possible in 15 minutes. You will then take a 1-minute break and then complete as many rounds of the exercises in segment 2 as possible in 15 minutes.

    a. Reps for each exercise: 11

    b. Segment 1 Exercises:

DUMBELL BENT OVER WIDE ROW

HIP EXTENSION

    c. Segment 2 Exercises

DUMBELL HIGH PULL

DUMBELL ROMANIAN DEADLIFT

SIDE PILLAR

4 Strength Workouts **Explained**

3. PUSH STRENGTH 2 – 15 MINUTE SEGMENTS

The concentration today's strength workout will be pushing exercises. Your goal is to complete as many rounds of the exercises in segment 1 as possible in 15 minutes. You will then take a 1-minute break and then complete as many rounds of the exercises in segment 2 as possible in 15 minutes.

    a. Reps for each exercise: 9

    b. Segment 1 Exercises:

DUMBELL STANDING OVERHEAD PRESS

WALL SIT

FRONT PILLAR

    c. Segment 2 Exercises

DUMBELL FLOOR PRESS

GOBLET SQUAT

---

4. PULL STRENGTH 30 MINUTE

The concentration of todays strength workout will be pulling exercises. We will complete a 5 exercise rotation as many rounds as we can complete in 30 minutes

    a. Reps for each exercise: 11

    b. Exercises:

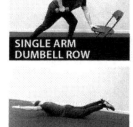
SINGLE ARM DUMBELL ROW

HIP EXTENSION

DUMBELL BICEP HAMMER CURL

SUPERMAN

DUMBELL ROMANIAN DEADLIFT

Exercise Pictures

PUSH UPPER BODY EXERCISES

1. Pushup

Level 1: On Knees

Level 2: On Feet

2. Dumbell Standing Overhead Press

Level 1: Low Weight

Level 2: Heavier Weight

Exercise **Pictures**

PUSH UPPER BODY EXERCISES

3. Bench Tricep Dip

Level 1: Knees 90°   *Level 2: Straight leg*   *Level 3: Legs elevated*

4. Dumbbell Floor Press

Level 1: Low weight   *Level 2: Heavier weight*

Exercise Pictures
PUSH LOWER BODY EXERCISES

1. Wall Sit
Level 1: Static with no weight

Level 2: Static with weight in goblet hold

2. Goblet Squat
Level 1: No weight goblet squat

Level 2: Weighted goblet

Exercise **Pictures**
PULL UPPER BODY EXERCISES

1. Dumbbell Bent Over Wide Row
Level 1: Low weight   *Level 2: Heavier weight*

2. Dumbbell High Pull
Level 1: Low Weight   *Level 2: Heavier Weight*

Exercise **Pictures**

PULL UPPER BODY EXERCISES

3. Dumbbell Bicep Hammer Curl

Level 1: Low weight

Level 2: Heavier weight

4. Single Arm Dumbbell Row

Level 1: Low Weight

Level 2: Heavier Weight

Exercise **Pictures**
PULL LOWER BODY EXERCISES

1. Dumbbell Romanian Deadlift
Level 1: Dowel

Level 2: Weighted

2. Hip Extension
Level 1: Double leg without weight

Level 2: Double leg with weight

Exercise **Pictures**

CORE EXERCISES

1. Front Pillar: 30 seconds - 60 seconds

Level 1: On knees

Level 2: On feet

2. Superman Hold: 30 seconds - 60 seconds

Resting position

Holding position

3. Side Pillar: 30 seconds - 60 seconds

Level 1: On knees

Level 2: On feet

MY STORY: PART 3

For the first time in my life since I was 16 years old, I was completely out of commission. It was a bit Earth shattering. A large part of my magic formula had been broken, along with several bones in my body. I figured a couple months and I would be good to start back slow. Here we are over two years later and I am still relatively crawling regarding the amount of movement restrictions I have. But you know what? It's all good. In fact, it's so good.

It's interesting because even though I call myself an expert, I forgot the fact that the smart experts still keep their eyes and ears open for learning experiences. It took me 1.5 years to finally say okay, we're not moving here. In fact, we are actually moving backwards. Time to make lemonade out of these lemons.

Like I said before, I took the accident as an opportunity to change the focus in my life to emphasize other areas. Did I plan on returning faster? Sure. However, I am grateful because the attention I was able to give to other areas of my life because of my understanding of FIT MIND enabled me to embrace this right from the start. The most important thing is that I'm back at it, and now I know better.

Overall, the accident gave me two very strong gifts of certainty in my profession and my life. The first is the power nutrition has in not only our body transformations but in life transformation itself. You can never out-train your nutrition and you most certainly cannot outrun your fork. The second is the necessity of frequent exercise to accelerate the body transformation process. These are two things that I know

now more than ever that I want as an integral part of my day-to-day life for the rest of my life.

After putting exercise back in, EVERYTHING accelerated literally right away. My first week back, I noticed a drastic change in my mood. I honestly didn't pay it too much attention until it actually continued to improve.

I began checking in and reflecting weekly to track more thoroughly how exercise was benefitting what is most important to me in my life. Four weeks in, my body was on its way but still needed much work for where I wanted to be. My life, however, was shooting straight up. I began to reflect on how my new actions were benefitting what is most important to me in life and it was so notable after four weeks. I remember saying to myself, "Man, I'm going to start writing this stuff down." What was going on was crazy.

It was clear as day. I had never separated exercise and nutrition from each other. Also, even if my nutrition was off at times over the years, I always exercised. Only when it was out of my daily regimen and suddenly put back in did the fire light up like a beast!

About two months back into my transformation, my body and, yes, all areas of my life were transforming right before my eyes. It was undeniable. I remember speaking with a friend about their own body transformation and I remember saying that first we need a fit mind; next we master a fit body. The two combined and applied consistently will lead to the fit life you are looking for. I immediately wrote the idea down because I knew what I had gratefully stumbled upon. Instantly, what you are reading was born.

It became very clear to me that if our fit body is not functioning at maximum capacity, how are we supposed to thrive in all other areas of our lives? How are we supposed to perform at the maximum level we are all capable of? How are we supposed to maximize the capacity of how we view ourselves? Our spiritual purpose? Our work success or any other area of life? We just can't. Armed with a fit mind, the transformation of the physical body is the greatest catalyst in transforming all other areas of life into a new orbit.

By feeding the body what it thrives on, we strengthen all cells, enabling them to rebuild, repair and function at a much higher capacity. When we eat unhealthy foods, it creates an acidic environment inside of our bodies and we immediately internally move into fight or flight mode, activating the sympathetic nervous system. Eliminating garbage from our diets, the body is no longer in an acidic state. We now activate our parasympathetic nervous system of digestion, rejuvenation and rebuilding, moving our bodies into an alkaline state, optimal for us to excel. By then training our bodies with short bouts of high-intensity exercise, we accelerate every cell, enabling them to become more efficient and effective in all of their processes.

The combination of fit mind and fit body together creates an environment to maximize the capacity in all areas of life. Over the past 22 years, I've had the privilege of being a part of thousands of transformations where I've observed this undeniably over and over again. But what makes me a true believer is witnessing it come to fruition in my own life. A fit mind plus a fit body is a life of confidence and certainty in ourselves in all areas of our lives. A fit mind plus a fit body equals a fit life.

FIT LIFE

The fit life is a life of rapid progress towards what we want to be, do and have in all areas of life.

Before we spoke about Dr. Demartini's seven areas of life and how each and every person has an individualized specific set of personal values that are most important to them in their lives. So how does this relate to a fit life? A fit life is defined as a life with goals and accelerated progress in all seven areas of life.

Sure, we can have goals in all areas with no progress. And yes, we can have goals in all areas with little progress. The fit life multiplies 10 times these results by putting everything into hyperdrive. Why? Because the fit life understands how our direct choices and actions impact what we value most in our lives and has earned us the ability to act more strategically. The end result is an incredible return on your investment.

For our fit mind, which is tied to the mental area of our lives, we identified what is most important to us. Doing this enables us to understand why we think, feel and act the way we do. If something supports what we love, we label it as good. And if something challenges what we love, we label it as bad. This shift gives us a whole new perspective on how we view everything, including ourselves. The closer we stay in alignment with our personal values, the greater our self-perception is and the greater our impact will be. We are now in line with what our heart wants for us, which is to fulfill our highest values.

Next, we went through the fit body, which is the physical area of our lives. Here, we learned the power of nutrition and exercise, which accelerates the actions of every single cell in our body. This loads the gun, enabling us to do everything we do at a much higher level.

So what about the other five areas of life? How are these transformed?

Previously, we spoke about all seven areas of life and quickly defined them for you. For review purposes, here is a quick run-through of the seven areas of life.

Spiritual is your relationship with God, or however you choose to define that. It is also how in line we are with living a life concentrated on our values by living out our purpose.

Mental is the fit mind and is all about personal growth and development. Yes, this can be scholarly development, but the root of our mental life is about our own self-perception, knowing what is most important to us in our lives, known as our highest values, and also understanding how our actions and inactions directly affect these same values.

Financial is monetary wealth, but it is also about our contribution potential. This is the amount of value we are able to add to people's lives at any given place and time.

Familial includes your immediate and extended family relationships in your life.

Vocational is your work, career or any hobbies you are involved with, contributing to your livelihood.

Social is your active involvement with your friends and others you associate with in social settings, personally as well as professionally.

Finally, the physical area of life is the fit body. This is our commitment to practicing all aspects of health, including but not limited to nutrition and exercise.

All of us inherently know what we want to be, do and have in all areas of life. The problem is that most have not defined that down on paper, nor do they revisit these goals and desires on a monthly, weekly or daily basis to keep them updated and at the top of their mind. Awareness is everything with our goals and desires. If we are not able to rattle off exactly what we desire in our lives in all areas of life, then we are simply not in control. Whenever we fail to govern ourselves, we become disempowered to the point where it will then be governed by another. It's time to take control because you deserve everything you want in your life.

People vary in their transformations according to their values of what they hold dearest to them. Some will have massive transformations in few areas with smaller transformations in other areas. It all depends where a person feels fulfillment or lack in their lives at the time they begin to transform. Whatever we perceive is most lacking, most missing or what we are most afraid to lose in our lives is what we value most and therefore what we pursue with our actions.

As I mentioned before, the definition of fulfillment is filling full that which we perceive is most missing or that we are most afraid to lose in our lives.

What would you say we want to fill in our lives with? That which we care most about or what we don't care about? What we care most about, right?

Fulfillment is about filling our desires surrounding our highest values. It just so happens that our highest values of what is most important to us in our lives are also what we fear losing most.

This explains to us exactly why we concentrate our time and energy on certain things and not others. It's the perfect personalized formula for all of us. Our values are structured around what we want to gain, what we want to keep, or what we are most afraid to lose in our lives. When we feel something is missing in our lives, or we desire to attain or maintain it, it is because it's what's most important to us. It is what gives us the most fulfillment in our lives. It fulfills what we perceive is most missing, what we want to keep, and it's also what we most fear losing

As we spoke about before, yes, you can have a fit mind and a semi-fit life without having a fit body. We can identify our values of what is most important to us in our lives. Doing this will give us the ability to look at everything in life and ask the question, "How is this a benefit or drawback to our highest values?"

Regardless of someone's values, having this knowledge will enable us to look at any and all areas of our lives, opening up a new line of communication, awareness and understanding. It enables us to look at all events occurring in life and assess how it is either a benefit or a drawback to what we hold dearest to us.

This is a huge step. However, there is only so far this will take us if we are missing the fit body. Transform the body, and everything we just spoke about goes to the next level. Our abilities to pursue what we love become maximized. Everything in all areas accelerates and is propelled forward faster, period.

Feeding our body what it thrives on and reinforcing that with challenging exercise creates an alkaline environment inside of us that's heightened, clearer, more focused and ultimately more capable of being a player rather than a spectator. Our body literally becomes a better version of itself down to a cellular level. We create an environment ready for growth, rather than one in fight or flight trying with everything it's got to merely hold the base together.

Let me ask you; if there were two other versions of you, one with just a fit mind pursuing the fit life and another version of you with a fit mind, practicing a fit body and pursuing a fit life, who would you put your money on and who would you want on your team?

MY TESTIMONIAL

Throughout the course of writing this book, I had the privilege and opportunity to sit down with many different people who wanted to share their stories with me of how a fit mind plus a fit body gave them a fit life. Let me tell you, the experience was inspiring, empowering, enlightening and humbling to say the least.

After you finish the conclusion of the book, be sure to continue on to read these incredible stories and experiences in the TESTIMONIAL INTERVIEW chapter. I wanted to separate the testimonial interview chapter from the rest of the book because of its significance.

This has been an amazing journey. I have discovered so much not only about myself but also how similar we all are. All of us have what is most important to us in our lives and all of us want to grow.

Personally, I'm blown away and in awe with what I have been able to experience thus far.

I am more relaxed than I have ever been because I feel my body is now functioning at maximum capacity. I am pushing myself continuously and leaving very little room for complacency. I feel like I'm running faster than ever and, ironically, I am more relaxed and filled with the joy of the process itself. I don't have the self-resentment of not doing what I say I want to do anymore because I am doing it. Little did I know, but my heart was telling me this the entire time. I just wasn't listening. I have beaten my fears that were attached with hitting this level and am now spreading my wings.

Spiritually, I am now in line with my purpose. Because of this, not only has my own self-worth exploded, but the value and worth I am able to provide others has also exploded. I now see myself as the leader I have been yearning to be. I have been given a gift. I grew up as an overweight kid constantly feeling disempowered. I found a formula for breaking down that boundary and I am hell-bent on sharing that with as many people as I can touch with it. I am now able to approach what I do with certainty and a lack of judgment of where anyone else currently is in their journey.

Mentally, the level of clarity, confidence, energy and efficiency I have gained is indescribable. It's like a light switch turned on and now I'm shining. I'm now firing on all cylinders in all situations both comfortable and uncomfortable.

This has been a perpetual growth and development experience for me, beginning with absolute inspiration. As soon as I began taking action towards getting my fit body back, I recognized that something was different in my mind. I was thinking differently about myself and this lit me on fire with inspiration. The cycle continued, leading to empowerment, accomplishment, more inspiration, more empowerment, more accomplishment, and the cycle continues rolling as I write this book.

Vocationally, I feel the best way I can describe this is that I am now thinking much bigger. The confidence I have gained through this has changed the way I view myself. I now know what I am capable of and, most importantly, I now believe in myself. The ceiling I had created over my own head has been lifted.

I have acquired a new business partner, which has been amazing. I am now surrounding myself with higher energy people. My business overall has exploded as we have more than doubled in size within the last year.

One of the greatest transformations I have been able to break through throughout my journey is that I am no longer sugar-coating situations with my team. I have committed to saying it exactly like it is. We all say we want to know if we are meeting the standards of the expectations around us so that we can grow, but the reality is that many will reject it when it is given. Not doing so leaves a situation where you find yourself surrounded by people who are dragging through life and not pushing the limits. We all need this to inspire us to our own next level.

Now, when expectations are not being met, I no longer tiptoe around the situation, I let the person know straight up. What I have learned is that I have been doing the people around me a disservice by not doing so. Every person wants to grow in some way, shape or form. If someone is doing something that is pushing them off of that path and we don't let them know, then what kind of mentor are we being for that person? The answer is a very poor one. In some cases, this has led to us parting ways with past team members, which has actually turned out to be a blessing. The truth is that cancer spreads and cancer kills. If there is one cancer cell in the mix, it will spread its energy to others. Removing this entirely has led to a much higher level of empowerment and inspiration throughout the rest of my team.

The certainty I now have in my work has come from the fact that I now am representing myself 100% prepared and deserving of where I am going and what I am out to accomplish. Where my body was in the past caused me to compare myself to others and perceive myself as not ready. Now I am ready and in hot pursuit.

Financially, I've set new personal standards of the value I want to be able to provide to others as well as the revenue I want access to in my life. Yes, I have a personal goal of being able to do whatever I want, whenever I want financially, but I never understood it. To be honest, I judged it. I thought, *Am I greedy?* Then I answered truthfully. *Yes.* I am just like every other human. I love serving others, and I also want the life I want in all areas, period, and I am willing to bust my ass to get it. We all desire certain things whether they be material, love, significance, recognition, or whatever it may be. What I've realized is the things I desire are all linked to better position me to fulfill my purpose.

I have big dreams. Many of these will take a significant amount of money to come true and I will not stand for green paper getting in my way of my goals and my purpose. Therefore, I'm dedicated to making sure I have access to what I need. Yes, that's right. I have a personal goal of being able to do whatever I want, whenever I want. Now I understand it and actually doing it is going to require my financials to be in order and ready to go because this will accelerate the entire process of what I want in my life. I know exactly what I want and I now am able to begin to quantify what doing that is going to cost. I've started formulating a plan to make sure it happens and I leave nothing to chance because, as all of us know, there is no chance in life, only choice. So I choose to plan, I choose to take massive action, and I will crush what I am here to do.

Familiarly, I have become a better leader and role model to the ones I love the most because I am not telling others what to do. I am simply leading by example. Just doing this has led them to also step out of their comfort zones and break through their own challenges.

My presence with my family has also improved by leaps and bounds. In the past, I was very distracted in family situations with other things I felt I needed to do. This affected my mood and my focus on my family. Now I am more efficient and effective in the other areas of my life and therefore am better able to be in the moment with my family.

My patience has been notably different not only with my family but across the entire board. I can see that this has everything to do with the lack of patience I was also displaying with myself. I was basically taking out my frustration with myself on the others around me. Not a pretty picture.

Overall, I am better able to serve those I love because I can focus on them better. I no longer feel like I am just holding on and surviving; I'm thriving and that better enables me to shine around those I love and even those I perceive as more abrasive to me.

Socially, my energy and vibration has changed. I am certain. I am confident. I am not distracted with myself and what others may be thinking about me. I am clear and ready to embrace those around me. I have a much greater level of acceptance for myself and, ironically, for others as well. When we love ourselves, we don't compare ourselves to others and hate on them for what they have and what they do not have. We are able to love others and appreciate them for who they are and where they shine. We become a "Go Giver", genuinely interested in serving others and lifting them up. Today, in social settings, I find myself thinking *Who in this room can I help?* When I was too distracted with my lack of satisfaction with myself, I was blind to this way of thinking. This same way of thinking has opened and continues to open doors I never had access to in the past.

Physically, my ultimate goal has been to be 195 pounds at 12% body fat year-round. Yes, this is a very direct and precise goal for a reason. For me, the power it holds drives everything else to a whole new level of living for me according to my values. Currently, as I write this, I am at 192 pounds and 11.5% body fat. I am just about there and will not stop once I get there. I already have my next set of goals ready to unleash. What I have learned about myself and others is that if we don't have something past our immediate goals to focus on with our body transformation, we lose our focus. Personally, I will not let this happen again. I have learned the lesson several times in the past, but this time was different. It was in my face and undeniable.

These realizations are what inspired me to write this book and share it with you in hopes that you too would benefit from it.

Previously, we spoke about the importance of consistency with transformation. Consistency is everything in the process. The beautiful thing is we are given the gift of choice to make this happen every single day. We either do or do not. There is no in between. This is why maintaining the clear connection with our highest values is crucial. We are then in a position where we can consciously understand how what we do and what we do not do directly impacts these same values.

"If we do something once successfully, it gets our attention. If we do it twice, it opens our eyes. If we do it every day, it changes our entire world." Trevor Buccieri

Just because the journey of this book is nearly complete, it is of utmost importance that we understand that the big picture of life transformation is never complete. It is an ongoing journey meant to be embraced and nurtured. The only way we are able to achieve this is through continual and consistent practice. This includes always being aware of our highest values and also through educating and feeding ourselves more inspiration to further accelerate our growth and development. I have had many people ask me what the one thing is I have done that has pushed me forward and I will say beyond a doubt it is education and filling my mind with inspiration each and every day. If I don't get my daily reading, I feel it and so does everyone around me.

CONCLUSION

The fit life is the life I believe each of us desires; a life of fulfillment led by directing all of our energies and actions towards that which we value most.

I'm not here to tell you that it's easy. In fact, I'm here to tell you it is the greatest challenge and gift we are all given: the opportunity to understand ourselves, to empower ourselves and to actually live the life of our dreams. This is the same life many people talk about like it's some kind of myth or unreachable peak. The takeaway to remember is that the greater the challenge we overcome, the greater the reward we receive in return. We never remember or truly appreciate the things that come very easy to us in life. On the other hand, the things that we struggle with the most, only to crash through in victory, are the same things we remember for the rest of our lives.

The beauty is that this picture is different and unique for every single person. I believe all of us have the ability to create exactly what we desire in our lives every day, beginning with the choice to either succumb to where you are or run towards where you want to be.

The interesting thing is that doing everything and doing nothing take the same amount of energy. It's simply distributed differently. The amount of anxiety we receive in our lives through the sense of lack and doing nothing far outweighs the energy it takes to bring constant action towards the life of our dreams every day.

Doing nothing creates a continual increase in self-doubt and lack in our lives, literally aging us in our own self-defeat.

Simply going for it at the new level turns on the turbo button and brings our own self-perception and development to new heights. Fall after fall, we get up again wiser and more capable than we were before the fall. Rinse and repeat over again consistently and the impossible has now just become possible.

FIT LIFE: TESTIMONIAL INTERVIEWS

I would love to take this opportunity to share with you several interviews of everyday people just like us, whose lives have been completely transformed through a fit mind plus a fit body. Every one of these people transformed their body, which has led to nothing short of miracles happening in all other areas of their lives. Their fit minds all recognize the significance transforming their bodies has added to their lives and why it is crucial for them to keep what they have earned. They realize that if it begins to slip away, all other areas begin to regress.

What I have been able to conclude through this experience with certainty is that it all comes down to what we think and feel about ourselves. When we love ourselves and can further develop our self-love, we become more open to love with everything and with everyone else in our lives.

Note:
Every person will have a different experience with their fit life transformation. We all have a unique snowflake specific set of values that we live our lives by, and therefore we all view experiences differently. We all have different goals and areas of focus in our lives, which are unique to us, so that only makes sense. What I found most interesting, though, were the many cross-correlations and similarities people experienced regardless of their values structures. I have found that we all have many similar desires; we simply view and express them differently.

When organizing the information from the interviews, I wanted to present you with an easy-to-follow format that would enable you to get to the heart of the takeaways without any waiting. That said, I used a simple question and answer format to keep things clear and organized. Enjoy!

Carmela

Carmela transformed her body by losing over 55 pounds.

Carmela, thank you so much for getting together with me today. I'm thrilled to be speaking with you today.

Carmela, what are your three highest values in order?

Family, health and spiritual.

What was your goal when you started your body transformation?

My goal when I first started Core Capacity was to get myself physically and emotionally healthy so I can better help my family.

Why did transforming your body become a must for you?

I had an accident with my knee and destroyed my ACL, MCL and both meniscus. I was approaching menopause and I found myself becoming depressed because I couldn't get up into the things I wanted to do, so in turn I gained more weight. Then I was in jeopardy of injuring my other knee. So, one day, I weighed myself and I wasn't just gaining two or four pounds in menopause, I was gaining 10. There I was at 4'11" and 190 pounds.

I wasn't sure what direction I should go to get out of that state. That's when I saw a friend with losing all this weight and I said, "What did you do?"

She said, "I go to Core Capacity."

I researched it then walked in one day and said, "I need to do this." I couldn't believe what I did in 12 weeks doing back-to-back challenges where I lost 47 pounds. My 50th birthday was right around the corner and I decided I wanted 50 and fabulous. So for my 50th birthday, I had lost 50 pounds and felt fabulous.

One day I woke up and the scales had jumped 10 pounds because I was no longer looking at it. I felt frozen. I felt like I couldn't move, like I couldn't breathe. I talked to my husband. I said, "I have to do something and I think this is it." I basically said, "Go big or go home." That's what I was going to do and there wasn't any going back from there. It changed my life, it changed my family's life, and it changed my friends' lives. In return, that constant feedback and positivity has only continued to make me feel better.

So let's talk about your transformation and the impact it's had on all areas of your life. What we teach is that the transformation of a fit mind and fit body together leads to accelerated transformation in all other areas of life. Let's break that down.

<u>How has your body transformation benefited your family relationships?</u>

Core Capacity has affected my family in a lot of different aspects. I think because I feel more confident and secure in my decisions and the general shopping, cooking, how it's affected how my daughter would eat as a teenage girl, how it affects my son. The other day, he comes up to me in my bedroom and says, "I made you a snack." It was apples and peanut butter. In the past, it would have been, "Mom, here's your diet Coke." Now it's to the point where with my family, my friends, and neighbors it's become a group thing. We are all inspiring and helping each other.

I am now the leader, the way I shop, the way we eat, the way we do everything. I've become the leader now in a positive role. With every household, let's keep it real, the mom is the mom and everything stems from that. My daughter eats healthier. My son eats healthier. The meals are better. I've learned so much from Core Capacity about how to eat healthy. It feels good to be that positive example now and not stuck in the world of like, "Oh my God, what am I going to do?" It's hard to explain because once you get that inside of you there is no going back and you're just like, wow, a weight was just lifted off.

When you feel like a leader, you feel empowered. Now you're empowered to move forward. You feel like you have the courage and you have the knowledge. My son would say to me, "Mom, you're healthy. I want to be healthy." That made me feel so good that I was having that impression on him.

It brought tears to my eyes because I felt good, but then I felt like, wow, I didn't realize in a sense the negative effect I was having on my family. You just get caught up going through the motions and just living life. Once I experienced this with my family, it made me feel like there is nothing that I can't do.

I know I'm not superwoman, but sometimes I wake up and feel like I am and that there is nothing I can't achieve because physically and emotionally I feel so strong. I feel like I have all the tools to do what I need to do and help my family and friends get there if, you know, they come and they would like my help.

Now, when we go to the beach, I'll go in the kayak and I'll race my daughter or I'll run on the beach. I can run with my son now. I can run with my dog. I didn't do these things before. I was afraid to do it before. Just seeing the difference in my daughter's face of "Wow, I'm proud of my mother." It feels so good to be a good example and just having my family proud of me. It's an amazing feeling where I am now as compared to where I was April 11th 2016. I think sometimes you have to get as low as low before you can break through.

Now let's talk about this on a scale of 1–10. On a scale of 1–10, how would you currently rate your family life?

My family life now is at a 10. I was at below a 0 myself. When you are physically and emotionally broken down, you can't help your family in any way. You can't even help yourself. Once I got past that point of my insecurities, my family life just heightened amazingly.

Where were you before your transformation on a scale of 1–10?

I was lucky to be a 1. I was pretty broken. Thank God I found the solution when I did. I don't know where I'd be if I didn't decide that today was the day to do it.

How has your body transformation benefited the physical area of your life?

Before I started Core Capacity, I was 4'11" and just under 190 pounds. I was struggling with a lot of emotions. I was going through menopause and had every side effect that you can have. When I decided to go to Core Capacity, I heard the stories of people who were adjusting their meds, whether they were diabetic or had heart issues or whatever. I would say it was by the end of my first six-week challenge, I stopped everything. I stopped the hormone supplements my doctor gave me. By the end of two challenges, which was 12 weeks, I had lost 47 pounds. I went to my doctor and he looked at my weight and he says, "Carmela you lost 50 pounds in this past year?" I said to the doctor that I'd lost 47 in 12 weeks and I'm not taking anything but vitamins and eating well. He said, "Good for you, Carmela." He could see the smile on my face. I was so happy to have a visit where I didn't get a printout that told me I was obese. I'm not afraid to go on the scale anymore. It's going down. It's not going up. I feel healthy and, mentally, I feel like I can accomplish anything.

When I looked back at my before picture with one of my trainers, Tom, he said to me sarcastically, "Oh my God, could you be any happier?" It looked like a mug shot, I looked that unhappy. It showed in my face that I was sad, and then in my after picture the smile on my face just said it all.

Where I am today, I have lost 55 pounds. Now when I go to the gym and listen to what we are doing that day, I sit Indian style and I couldn't do that before. I couldn't bend my knees that way. When Rick and I go to a show, I'm short so my feet don't reach the ground. Now I sit Indian style.

I look to myself like, *Wow, when was the last time you could sit Indian style?* It just makes me feel good. I love to do skater hops because I couldn't do it before with my knees. I couldn't do box jumps. Now I can. My body can physically do it where I don't feel like I'm going to blow my nose or hurt my back.

Physically being able to do things that you couldn't do directly affects you emotionally. It's hard to explain how inside you feel that you've accomplished something so simple that you couldn't accomplish before. It's not just okay. Physically, I can jump and my knees are better because the weight's been taken off. Emotionally, it takes away the fear.

Fear itself held me back. The fear that I want to be lying in bed worried about where I'm going to be and how the weight is going to affect me emotionally and physically. Lifting the fear off of me in a sense takes away the fear of menopause. It kept me scared. I felt like I was being crushed. So every little accomplishment that I've chipped away at has opened up my world so much.

Since I started in 2016 and now we're in September of 2017, I feel like I crushed it. I said I'm not going to do this anymore, it's not going to control me, but it was. Losing the weight helped so much physically and emotionally that I was able to go off the meds. I was able to just stop. I said, "I don't want to do this anymore."

Now let's talk about this on a scale of 1–10. On a scale of 1–10, how would you currently rate the physical area of your life?

I would say I am a 9. Every day I fill out your mood and food tracker. I looked back for the past few months, my mood has always been an 8 to 10 and, physically, it's also been an 8 to 10. In the past, it was maybe a 2 and some days a 4.

Where were you before your transformation on a scale of 1–10?

I was a 3.

How has your body transformation benefited you spiritually?

Spiritually, since I started Core Capacity, I have made some very big progress. Every day I fill out my mood and food tracker at the beginning and end of the day. Let's say I fill out my tracker in the morning and I am an 8 today. Then by the end of the day maybe I'm a 10. I ask myself the question, "Why are you a 10 right now?" Now I can get a better understanding of what I did to get that. The positivity, the health, the emotional, the physical and the spiritual are all tied together. I feel like I have more control. I feel like I'm more in touch with myself. I don't know if that sounds crazy to people but, hey, I don't care. I feel like I'm more of a whole person. I feel fuller.

I have the confidence of losing the weight. To me, that was what held me down. I felt like I wasn't comfortable in my own skin and that's everything. That's emotional, that's spiritual. It was holding me back. To me, I felt like I wasn't a good person. I don't know why. That's not everybody's feeling. You just feel like you're not put together yet. There are pieces of you all around. Once you get all those pieces together, however, that works for you or however your goals work for you just nitpicking at just each one, it just encompasses the whole body and it feels amazing.

This is lifetime for me. I found my niche. I found what works for me in my life, my family and everything else. I don't know how to explain it, but it works for me.

Now let's talk about this on a scale of 1–10. On a scale of 1–10, how would you currently rate the spiritual area of your life?

On a scale of 1 to 10 spiritually, I'm probably about a 7. There is still some soul searching I need to do for myself and I think that's just part of the goals that I haven't crushed yet. This has definitely opened the door for me to be able to do that.

Where were you before your transformation on a scale of 1–10?

Probably about a 1 or 2. I felt pretty broken back then.

How has your body transformation benefited you mentally?

Mentally, it was destroying every bit of my life. I would go to work, come home and basically just get by, but I was falling into depression because I didn't like how I felt. I didn't like what I couldn't do. I didn't ride my bike with the kids anymore; I didn't run around the block. I would follow my son in the car because he has special needs and he wanted to ride his bike. That's how sad I felt.

I think mentally, since I started Core Capacity, everything has been enabled for me. I felt like I was a piece of the room. I didn't feel like I was actually a part of the room. I was kind of in the back. I didn't go forward. I didn't have the confidence. I didn't have the self-esteem that I now have. When you feel good about yourself as a whole, whether it's physical, spiritual or mental, it shows in your face. It shows in your body. I feel six feet tall sometimes and I know I'm never going to get there, but I do. I feel like I can conquer the world. I feel like I can conquer today no matter how hard it is. Back when I started, when I was full-blown menopausal, there were days I didn't get out of bed. I would think, *Hell no, am I going to go to a gym, or lose weight, or be able to get past this?* It was so crippling for me that I didn't see an out. I didn't know that I could feel an 8 or 10 because I never thought about it that deep until I got there. Now I feel great and I can't wait to see what tomorrow brings and to set my next goals even higher.

The confidence that I've acquired since I've been at Core Capacity has made me approachable. I guess your perception of yourself really affects how others perceive you. I feel good that people have approached me, not just because of the weight loss but also because of the whole package of who I am now. Sure, they see the physical, but once you talk to them and pick up how they are looking at you, you realize it's everything. It's how you view yourself that determines how others look at you.

Now I'm not only helping myself, I'm also helping others. I bring people into the gym as a guest and many are really scared. I'm able to help them through and knowing that I am able to help them just feels good. Now I can do that with them and for them, when before I felt like I couldn't even do it for myself. Now I am helping my family. I can do it for my son, daughter and husband and feel good about myself at the end of the day. Not because of what the scale says but because of what it gave back to me in my entire life.

I can't even tell you how many people have approached me that I have been able to help. They say, "But I'm a diabetic," or, "I have high blood pressure." I tell them that there is nothing I haven't seen and been able to help people get through just like they helped me, if you just follow the program. I was not expecting it, and even though the program is not specifically designed to help with menopause, it did. I know that sounds crazy to some people, but it helped me get there. Seeing people get these same leaps in their lives makes me feel so good that I was able to help that person.

I think the transformation most of all has enabled me to be real and honest with people because I'm not holding anything back. I would never tell anybody my weight as a woman. I would never talk about menopause. I felt like it was killing me, but now, because I crushed it, I feel good about it. I feel like the fears are gone. I feel like the confidence is there and feeling good, I think, is the start to anything moving forward. If you don't feel that you're confident about your beliefs and your goals then you're really not going to go anywhere.

Now let's talk about this on a scale of 1–10. On a scale of 1–10, how would you currently rate your life mentally?

Today, I feel like a 10, but I'm never lower than an 8.

*Where were you before your transformation on a scale of 1–
10?*

Before, I was a 1 or 2. I really feel great. I feel like this place
has really turned my life around for me, my family, my
lifestyle, and everything about me.

No other gym or weight loss center touches you like that, but
this place did. I was up front and I remember somebody
saying, "It's like a counseling session in here." I just listened
and it really is. It's a counseling session of what are you
going to do today or somebody has an injury. Maybe
somebody can't work out tomorrow or they're laid off for
weeks because they hurt themselves. They are still able to
come in and move forward with modifications even when
they are restricted. They are still there. I had to have surgery,
but I went as soon as I was allowed because, emotionally, I
knew I needed to walk in there. The time away was killing
me because it's more than just a gym. It's more than just
physical for me, it's emotional.

How has your body transformation benefited you financially?

I have never put a price tag on health. Rick and I said from
the beginning that it's not price, it's not money, it's whatever
the stakes, whatever we have to do; you will be lifetime
member. I want to be able to afford going to Core Capacity
really. That's my biggest thing.

What has changed is my contribution value. It's remarkable.
What a huge difference. One of my neighbors was recently
over and she was so grateful that I took the time to talk to her
and help her. I was able to talk to her and help her. She said,
"I'll never forget the day I was over at your house and I told

you I needed surgery in a month. You said, 'What are you waiting for? Start now.'" Then she started. She just sent me a Christmas card thanking me for that. It made such a difference in her life and the reward of that is huge now. Yes, I have my big goals for this coming year, but to be able to bring that to others is amazing.

The value I am able to bring to others is tenfold. It's amazing; the support I'm now able to give and also receive in return is night and day. Without a level of self-worth in your own life, you don't have the confidence to think that you can guide somebody else.

She told me she was going to have to have surgery soon and I told her not to wait, start right now.

Now let's talk about this on a scale of 1–10. On a scale of 1–10, how would you currently rate your life financially?

I would say a 9 or 10. The confidence I have going into new things and what I can do for others is completely different than it was before.

Even just last night, I went to the Y with my daughter and I was showing her different core movements because she really wanted to work on that. It just felt so good to be able to teach my 17-year-old different things that were going to help her where she wanted help.

Where were you before your transformation on a scale of 1–10?

It was a 2. It was very low. I went through some very tough times before I started.

How has your body transformation benefited your work life?

I think my transformation has impacted me physically to do a better job at work. I feel like I have more energy and I don't feel like in the middle of the day I want to take a nap. I guess it gives me the "I can accomplish anything" attitude. The job doesn't seem as difficult when you have energy and confidence. Whether it's a meeting, or you have to approach somebody face-to-face, you feel good about yourself.

I'm also much more efficient at work and, honestly, everywhere in life. I start my day at 5:30 a.m. and with my home life, kids, dog, working out and working, I don't feel I'm exhausted by the end of the day. Before, I didn't have that energy. I didn't even think I could get out of bed sometimes.

When I didn't have the energy, the motivation, the confidence, the security in myself, by the time I finally got home at the end of the day, I was not a happy camper. It was affecting me and my family. Emotionally, if you're torn down, you're going to affect everyone else in your household.

Now let's talk about this on a scale of 1–10. On a scale of 1–10, how would you currently rate your work life?

Now, I feel like I am a 9 or 10. I feel excited about the challenges we have ahead because I'm more confident in myself.

Where were you before your transformation on a scale of 1–10?

Before I was a 4 or 5.

How has your body transformation benefited the social relationship area of your life?

Socially, since I've been at Core Capacity, of course, I want to do more. I'll go out to music and Main, and I'll go out there and dance, where before I wouldn't do such a thing. I wouldn't be out there taking pictures or be the one in the middle of the crowd dancing with my daughter and acting silly. Physically, I didn't feel good about myself. At this point, I also feel that I'm a positive role model for others and especially my children.

I feel like being more relaxed as I am now is opening me up to things that I never even knew existed. Sometimes, you don't know what's out there because you're so afraid to approach it, but when you put yourself out there, I truly believe that you soak in that positivity from others. It becomes a part of you. There's a reason you come across everybody you meet in life. They have an impact in some way on your emotional growth as you go on. When you feel insecure and you're not out there, you have no idea what you're missing because you have no idea what's there. This has definitely enabled that for me.

Now let's talk about this on a scale of 1–10. On a scale of 1–10, how would you currently rate your social life?

Socially, on a scale of 1–10, I am a 10.

I was maybe a 3? I was the one behind the picture. I was the one peeking like this because I didn't want anyone to see, you know, how short I looked, how wide I looked or how overweight I looked.

The heart of my philosophy is that the transformation of the mind and body together leads to accelerated transformation in all other areas of life. Do you agree, and what are your thoughts on that?

I totally agree with that. I think one paralyzes the other if you don't have them both and if they don't grow together.
Don't you?

1,000% I do.

When your mind is there and your body is there, it just works. My mind is a very powerful thing and when I was at my lowest, it really crippled me. My body transformation has taken it to a new height for me.

It would have never gotten to this point where I could say that I am excited about the challenging goals that I set for myself within the next year. I'm actually excited because I know I am going to do this. I am going on a cruise in March, so I'm excited to go from where I am now to where I will be then. Where I will be mentally through the challenge and, of course, what I will look like physically.

Before I started Core Capacity, it was all about lose 20 pounds in six weeks. I thought, *Okay, I can do this.* Then I wanted more because I felt great. I did another six-week challenge back to back and that was 47 pounds. I realized then it wasn't about the weight. There was something else. I wanted to still lose 50 pounds by the time I was 50 and I did that, which was big to me. Then I realized again that it isn't about the 50 pounds anymore. It's about everything it gave me, everything I took from it, and everything it took away. It took away the fear. It gave me confidence and I'm not just talking about the physical confidence, it gave me the emotional stability that I was lacking.

Transformation to me means total embodiment. It's the transformation of the body and your soul. You transform your entire life not just your physical. And I never thought about it that much when I was doing my challenges until one day I walked into the gym and I'd see everybody's physical transformation on the wall and I'm, like, *Okay, their physical body is transformed.* Now, about a year and a half later, I realize that it totally transformed my soul. Everything about what I think, eat, do, how I live, where I go, my activities, it transformed everything for me.

I am grateful for everything this place had to offer me then and continues to offer me every day. I can say now that I'm definitely living the life that I want to live and I'm excited about tomorrow. I'm not afraid. I now have the knowledge of what to do and how to do it moving forward.

Did the values and goal-setting exercise help you through your transformation? If so how?

Definitely. I've actually taken it even further for myself. I have taken all of my challenges that I have done and incorporated them into my everyday nutrition.

I have also written down everything transformation means to me and continually read that and say that back to myself. I'm also a firm believer in writing things down when I struggle. Many times I'll be writing down the fact that I didn't have the extra cookie. So it's not just the good actions I took but also the choices I made to stay away from certain things as well. I'm tracking my accomplishments.

Do you feel that the information it gave you will help you keep your results?

Yes, I have no doubt that I will never go back. I will never go backwards. I'm not scared. It's now more exciting to see what's going to happen.

Tom

Tom transformed his body by losing over 80 pounds and 12% body fat.

Tom, thank you for joining me today, man. It's really great to have you. I'm really excited to hear your story.

Tom, what are your three highest values in order?

My three highest values are family, health and my social relationships.

What was your goal when you started your body transformation?

When I walked in, I was at my low. Bottom line, my first goal was really to just get through the first workout. My second goal was to transform my body into something myself and my family could be proud of. I did not like where I was at whatsoever. I didn't want to go out anymore. I was changing my clothes three times before I would because I didn't want to look like a sausage case, you know?

Why did transforming your body become a must for you?
If you remember, when I walked through that door, I was over 300 pounds. Even at that point, my brain was really good at tricking me. I could still look in the mirror and say, "It's not that bad."

So my mom, one Mother's Day leading up to that June before I made my move, pulled me aside and said, "I don't want to lose you." That was the final straw for me. I do what I do, but hearing it from her for the first time ever was the deciding factor. It was a poignant moment and, I kid you not, I can still hear it like it was yesterday.

So let's talk about your transformation and the impact it's had on all areas of your life. What we teach is that the transformation of a fit mind and fit body together leads to accelerated transformation in all other areas of life. Let's break that down.

How has your body transformation benefited your family relationships?

You know that's a funny one. That is actually the most painful one that we will be touching on today. I say that because I'm in an unfortunate situation right now. I am in the middle of splitting up with my wife. Now, I have been married now for 24 years and there were issues along the way for sure. The goal here, though, was to be better, be healthy and make my kids proud. I did all that. This situation just turns out to be what it is.

The truth is that this did not only help me, but it actually also helped my wife as well. It did have a positive effect on the family for sure. It's just a bit hard dealing with this current challenge. That said, if I were in the same situation that I am now with my wife and I was still over 300 pounds that could have put me over the edge to be honest.

Coupled with the sadness of this, along with the disappointment of looking in the mirror, would have been much worse.

This has made a huge difference for me. I'm looking at going into a new chapter of life. It's so much better to go into a new chapter feeling good about yourself rather than feeling absolutely horrible and completely sad. I mean, wow, it's been huge for sure in helping me get through this.

With my kids, it has made quite a difference. I had let myself go and I wanted my kids to be proud of me. I feel the biggest things that have helped our relationship overall have been the changes in my mood, my mindset and my confidence.

When you are not feeling yourself, you hide yourself. You feel sad and disappointed in yourself. I found myself in a place where I was angry because I felt like there was nothing I could do about it and that just isn't me. In fact, when I was talking to my daughter about this, she actually said, "That was the angry years, Dad," and I was like man I didn't know that. That's just not who I am.

With my mom before this transformation, her biggest fear was making sure I was going to be able to take care of things. If something happens to me, what is going to happen to her, you know? Now, she has the confidence that I am going to be around and it makes her life much better.

I love my mom. She did everything for us and now it's our turn to give back. To be able to juggle my busy schedule and fit her in is huge. I wanted to make sure I was able to take care of my family, run my business, and make sure I get my time with her so I can look in her eyes to make sure she is okay. Again, the energy is just there to me and I realize now just how much I've wanted it.

Now let's talk about this on a scale of 1–10. On a scale of 1–10, how would you currently rate your family life?

I'd say an 8.

Where were you before your transformation on a scale of 1–10?

Struggling, in pain at a 5.

How has your body transformation benefited the physical area of your life?

Before I started my transformation, I went to the doctor to see where I was at. I was over 300 pounds at that point. When my tests came back, everything was perfect except my sugar was on the high side of normal. This came as no surprise considering I was eating, like seven candy bars per day. This was the moment I could have said that I have been trying to kill myself the past 10 years. Why not take this get-out-of-jail-free card and go for it? I didn't do that for another year.

Now when I go into my doctor, he is raving. He says, "Look at your weight. Look at your numbers."

The health area has been dramatic for me and that means a lot to me. I don't like the idea of being a time bomb that is ticking away. The fact that, to the best of my ability, I am being proactive ... it keeps me smiling.

Keep me out of the system. I am not a good person in the system and if I can keep doing things to avoid that, believe me, I am going to do it.

Even down to the simplest stuff, man. It all starts with being able to just put your clothes on without feeling like you are cutting off the circulation in different parts of your body. It starts there.

Being able to go out and buy clothes at any store versus having a very limited choice. Before I came to you, I was up to a 44-inch waist and triple x shirts. Now I am at a 36-inch waist very comfortably and just an extra-large shirt. It's such a different feeling being able to go into Gap and buy jeans and a belt.

Going out and having people look at you. Those who haven't seen you in a while say, "Wow." They recognize and respect the work that you've done. It's a good feeling. I mean, I don't have to be stroked necessarily, but hey, it doesn't hurt, right?

Tom, I 100% agree man.

Now let's talk about this on a scale of 1–10. On a scale of 1–10, how would you currently rate the physical area of your life?

Honestly man at this point I'm pretty pumped about it. I would say a 9.

You know you have busted your ass man. I always say there are people who expect results to just happen and those that make results happen. That now is you, my friend.

I really appreciate that.

You know going from a ranked athlete to all of a sudden becoming an absolute slob, it has taught me again to push through. Even when it hurts, even when you feel like you can't, even when you feel it isn't going to work out, you just keep pushing through man.

Where were you before your transformation on a scale of 1–10?

It was a 4. I was not in a good place. It did not make for a happy guy, that's for sure.

How has your body transformation benefited the social relationship area of your life?

It's been good. It's funny because, at this point in my life, I'm actually trying to almost repair relationships because I went into hiding. My whole thought process was if I don't have it figured out at home, I don't want to export it. With that, I found myself just staying away from my buds. I have talked with some of my good friends and basically said, "Hey it wasn't you, guys. I'm sorry that I kept blowing you off." Now that it's out, it's been great to get it off my chest and move forward to re-establish these precious relationships.

Let me ask you if you were not in the physical situation that you are right now would you be able to do that?

Mmm... Man, I will tell you what. It could be pretty dark right now, Trevor, I can tell you that. I would say absolutely not man. It would be bad. I feel like I am much better prepared to handle and deal with this now.

Now let's talk about this on a scale of 1–10. On a scale of 1– 10, how would you currently rate your social life?

It's definitely good man. I would say it's an 8.

Where were you before your transformation on a scale of 1– 10?

I'm going to have to again say a 4.

How has your body transformation benefited you spiritually?
I would say in reference to my belief as a Christian, if you believe that your body is a temple and that you have been polluting it for quite a long stretch, if you were to begin to take care of it so you can build the energy to give more, then it's a step in the right direction. I mean that is really the minimum. I have spent a lot of time in Bible studies, leading them and reading the Bible. Bottom line is that you can know a lot and you can internalize a lot, but you have to be out

there authentically with your hand out and your smile on. That is what is going to change people and change the situation. Without the confidence, energy and passion, you are a loud thought, but there is no noise. That's all I feel about it any way.

Even though I rate this the same because of some really deep convictions, it has helped in all of this. It has given me strength to pull through the sadness and challenge I have gone through.

Now let's talk about this on a scale of 1–10. On a scale of 1–10, how would you currently rate the spiritual area of your life?

In all honesty, it still suffers because of other areas of my life. I'll give it a 6 today and it needs to get back to a 10.

Where were you before your transformation on a scale of 1–10?

Oh gosh, before this? Well, unfortunately, that has been in a bit of a holding pattern, so I will go with 6. From the practical standpoint, it is good, but there need to be some more fundamentals put back into it and following a closer path.

I feel like I'm in a position to give more, but I feel that I am more out of practice. My potential is greater; now it's just time to move forward.

How has your body transformation benefited you mentally?

I would say that I had no clue that you could be sharper if you were not eating as much garbage. I didn't believe that. I always counted on my intellect and my wit. Now I will say there is no doubt. With more energy, more focus, I'm sharper and I would say I am as good as ever as we are sitting here today from a mental standpoint. Just my confidence alone. From the minute you get up, you can look at yourself and you can brush your teeth without shit jiggling all over the place. You can get into the shower without being a sloppy mess. I mean everybody has work to do, but just the improvement you know? It's actually funny you mentioned it. I have a picture hanging on the wall in my office of me playing golf in 2009. My assistant just pointed it out the other day recognizing how far I have come. She said, "That picture is what you need to remember. You have done so much and come so far. Most importantly, you have held on to it." I probably looked at that picture about five more times that day and thought, *Damn that was a tragic time.*

What I have really learned through my transformation is that I just can't let it go. Not that you can't go off every once in a while. It comes down to doing yourself a huge favor and you hold on to it and keep it going. You put all this work in, then you go back to your old habits and, before you know it, you are back up 10 pounds. Then you run into the risk of your old brain turning back on where you begin to justify it. Just a vicious circle back down.

In April, I felt myself creeping again. I began to see it in my clothes and in the mirror. And even though when this was happening, I could go in the gym for 40 minutes and kill it, it didn't mean it was going well. I then pushed myself right down near to my all-time low weight. After the challenge I am doing now, I will be at my all-time low. That was another reason I joined the challenge I am doing now, because I wanted to get to my all-time low and then see what I can do from there.

The biggest thing I have gained from your program is that I've found a foundation to grab on to that gives me hope and faith and keeps me on the track I want to be on.

Now let's talk about this on a scale of 1–10. On a scale of 1–10, how would you currently rate your life mentally?

I'd say it's really good. It's a 9.

Where were you before your transformation on a scale of 1–10?

It was pickled. It was sloshing around at a 5.

The truth is now in the gym setting, in that family setting, I have never felt better. I have never been more able to give. I've never felt as much of a leader as I do. It's really great stuff.

How has your body transformation benefited you financially?

Well, honestly, over the past several years, the growth has kind of coincided with my transformation. It's been kicking ass! Really because of timing and because of my fine physique, I am killing it. Seriously though, with my mental change and my confidence boost, it has made a very big difference. There is no question about it. With my business, it is a dressed-up business. You want to look sharp and look like you are taking care of everything all the time. Perception is reality as it is in life and certainly in the business I'm in.

Of course, I try to keep it real as much as possible, but there is still an expectation and you want to look good. People gravitate towards things that look good and make them feel good. Truthfully, it has been big.

Now let's talk about this on a scale of 1–10. On a scale of 1–10, how would you currently rate your life financially?

I would say it is a 9.

Where were you before your transformation on a scale of 1–10?

I would say it was a 6.

How has your body transformation benefited your work life?

I think it's changed in the idea that people respect you more. They see the hard work you are putting in. Not only do they respect you for what you know, and the person that you are, which is huge, on top of that, when you stack that with hard work, dedication and results, you can definitely see it in the way people perceive you, act towards you and respect you. It definitely has changed for the better.

Then, of course, I'll be on a trip or at a meeting and run into a colleague of mine I've known for years who lifts me up by saying what a great job I've done. So I think two things are happening there. One, they are respecting me and, two, hopefully I'm encouraging them. If I can do it, step up; you can do it too.

One of the biggest perceptions in the working world is that if you are fat then you are lazy. This has really helped make me a better person because, before this, I was that guy. Even though I was really overweight, fat, I was still killing it. I was still out there cutting my lawn and helping my neighbor. I was trying to debunk that even though I couldn't control what people thought of me. I look at people who come in here when they first start and I think, *Yes, you are really trying hard.* They just have the right idea. They are just willing to do it and try through it all. I love it because they are in there to push their own limits. Seeing that makes me go harder, I'll tell you that.

Now let's talk about this on a scale of 1–10. On a scale of 1–10, how would you currently rate your work life?

I would rate it an 8. When I can get my brain fully straightened out here, it'll be back at a 10.

Where were you before your transformation on a scale of 1–10?

I'll give it a 6. I never was too far off my game, but, like I said, there's a lot more to it when you are hiding.

The heart of my philosophy is that the transformation of the mind and body together leads to accelerated transformation in all other areas of life. Do you agree, and what are your thoughts on that?

I 100% agree with that. My thoughts are that I look back at my life with all the decisions I've made, the failures and successes, I was never able to pull together the physical area with everything else I had accomplished. I thought if I could just pull this area together and be happy with what I look like, that would be the final piece. Of course, as fate would have it, of course, it's never that easy, but I can assure you that it is huge. It's always been that stumbling block for me. Even though I was able to excel athletically, and be recognized for different things, the idea was that I always knew I could do so much better if I were stronger. If I had a bit more endurance, I could really kill it. Maybe instead of being number two, I could be number one.

I know I've been a bit long-winded here, but I will tell you that it absolutely, positively makes a huge impact. It doesn't change everything as you go, but I will tell you what, it better prepares you to fine-tune whatever you are focusing on.

Did the values and goal-setting exercise help you through your transformation? If so, how?

It did. Honestly, I'm not a great process guy. I'm really good at being out there, testing things out and correcting along the way.

The direct answer is, yes, it really does, because of the fact that life is hard. When you look back at why you do this, it makes sense. I hear members and challengers encouraging each other when they doubt themselves. They say, "Look back at your book. Why did you start this to begin with?" People come up with every excuse in the book from "I'm hurt," to "This is too hard, I don't think I'm going to make it."

At this point, my brain doesn't work like that. I see that it's 3 p.m. and it is just time to go and work out! Unfortunately, I have a hard time looking back and it's so important. I want to get better at that. You can see and appreciate the change so that you can relish it a bit more rather than always be in top gear. I couldn't agree more. It's really critical to be able to look back and believe that you can make it happen.

Do you feel that the information I gave you will help you keep your results?

Yes. Once you can internalize it and believe you can do it, it's about just doing it. Like I said, it's hard to stay on track because there are so many distractions in this world. For me, it always goes back to keeping an eye on it. When it comes down to it, if you don't know, then you don't know. I always try to bring it down to bite-sized pieces. For me to thrive, it has to be something real tangible I can put my arms around. If I thought of it, believe it and have put it down, it really helps keep me on track.

Laura

Laura transformed her body by losing 10 pounds and 5% body fat.

Laura, I wanted to start by saying I appreciate your time today. For those of you who don't know, Laura is my wife. She is one of my greatest inspirations and to see her sitting here after all of the hard work she has put in makes me proud.

Laura, what are your three highest values in order?

So right now the number one is my family. Number two is keeping the house and the kids and everything in order, and then number three would be health.

What was your goal when you started your body transformation?

I definitely wanted to lose weight and I guess achieve a certain look. I also wanted to become more confident and grow. I was sick of hiding my body under my clothes and was feeling embarrassed about it, even though other people didn't notice as much because it's not like I was huge or anything, but I noticed and just didn't feel confident.

You weren't able to be like your true self?

100%. I wanted not to have to worry about that aspect of things. I wanted that to be under control so I could focus on other things I want to do.

Why did transforming your body become a must for you?

It's because I could tell it was affecting areas of my life that were really important to me like taking care of the kids, and being with you. I didn't have enough energy. I was tired and definitely got frustrated a lot easier. I was craving food that was not good for me and then just giving in to it and feeling ashamed I guess, you know? I felt defeated. You can't put as much into the people you love because you're not happy with yourself. I didn't feel clean, I didn't feel healthy and I was like, "This has to stop now," because I could feel it spiraling. I was really getting frustrated at the kids and snapping at them more and probably snapping at you and wasn't confident. I wanted to be happy and I wasn't.

So let's talk about your transformation and the impact it's had on all areas of your life. What we teach is that the transformation of a fit mind and fit body together leads to accelerated transformation in all other areas of life. Let's break that down.

How has your body transformation benefited your family relationships?

Just so much. I mean like I was saying before how I didn't feel energetic and was getting frustrated and cranky a lot with the kids. Now it's so much different. I can wake up and feel clear and energetic and be ready for the day instead of waking up with a food hangover and cranky every day. Now I'm starting the day ready for whatever. Ultimately, it's a better day in general with the kids, you, and whatever we're going to do together. I feel clean and I don't have food hindering and clouding my mind and body because that's what it was doing.

You could feel it?
Oh my gosh. Every day and all day. And every time I would feel it, I would think about it. Now I'm not thinking about it. I have room in my head for everything else I'm doing. Now I'm in control of it and I feel so much better.

Now let's talk about this on a scale of 1–10. On a scale of 1–10, how would you currently rate your family life?

I would say 10. I love my family and I think we're even more awesome now.

Where were you before your transformation on a scale of 1–10?

Ugh… 5 or 6?

I mean not that we didn't have a good family life. It was good, but it wasn't where I potentially could be. Now it's great!

How has your body transformation benefited your work life with taking care of the kids, me, and the household?

It comes down to the fact that I am on top of it instead of letting it bury me and being in control of me. I have more energy to multi-task and get things done faster. I think more clearly. Making lists, charts, calendars and keeping it all in order makes me just a happier mom, which in turn makes a happier husband and kids. I thrive on organization and it's helped me be so much more organized because, again, my body isn't clouded, and my mind isn't clouded. It just helps me have so much more energy. I can keep up with the kids and what I do for you. It's a lot to keep up with and keep track of everything. I feel like when I'm clean, I'm on top of it all. Before, I felt like I was failing. I was just being lazy and putting off the things I wanted to do. Now I just do it.

Now let's talk about this on a scale of 1–10. On a scale of 1–10, how would you currently rate your work life?

I would say 9 you know? I don't think I would give myself a 10 because there is always room for improvement.

Where were you before your transformation on a scale of 1–10?

Maybe a 6?

That's like gaining a 50% increase in your performance every day.

Exactly. To me, living a 6 was like taking the backseat. Where I am now is rewarding for sure.

How has your body transformation benefited the physical health area of your life?

I didn't have health problems before. So it's not in a medical way, but I think just physically being stronger makes me feel just so empowered. Not having to ask you or anyone to help me lift something. I love feeling independent and I think this has helped my independence. Feeling stronger, more energetic and vibrant, looking better, just all that stuff is just different. I've reached some highs through this where I'm like, "I don't think it could get any better than this," and it's the best feeling in the world to feel like that. I don't feel worried about going to my next check-up. I know I'm healthy and it's great to know that and feel that.

I feel so much lighter like I can take anything on. Bigger things don't seem as big because emotionally I'm not weighed down as much.

I even have been getting better sleep. I love the feeling of waking up in the morning and not being tired. It's not like I'm jumping out of bed, but I get up and I'm awake and I'm ready for the day and I have energy. I'm not sluggishly walking to the bathroom. Now I'm ready.

Now let's talk about this on a scale of 1–10. On a scale of 1–10, how would you currently rate the physical area of your life?

I really think that I have reached a point at times where I felt like a 10. I don't know, I guess I'll say 9 because there's always room for improvement with it. I don't want to say I'm perfect, but there are times when I've felt like "Wow, I can't feel better than this."

Where were you before your transformation on a scale of 1–10?

My God, like a 4.

When I hit my low, it was a tomorrow situation. It happened over a couple of months. Not like I was feeling amazing before that, but I think the deterioration of that was the holiday season and it really hit me then.

It doesn't take long when it's time.

How has your body transformation benefited you spiritually?

You and I have very similar spiritual beliefs, if not the exact same. I think going right to purpose, I felt such a clear sense of that after my transformation. I felt more at peace with everything too. A lot of my worries had gone away. I'm a naturally anxious person, so I felt much more peace with what I was doing, what we were doing and everything. I feel like I'm doing exactly what I want to do and I'm fulfilled. I don't feel like I'm missing out on everything. I feel like I'm doing what I'm here to do and it makes me not feel anxious about it anymore.

I think when you're in the other state, you are always reaching for other things you think will make you happy and they don't because really it comes from within you.

Now let's talk about this on a scale of 1–10. On a scale of 1–10, how would you currently rate the spiritual area of your life?

I would say 9.

Where were you before your transformation on a scale of 1–10?

Like a 6. You know nothing before was terrible. It was good, but it was stagnant. Now it feels like it skyrocketed.

How has your body transformation benefited you mentally?

Well, I know I've said this a bunch of times, but I'll say it again. The mental clarity that I have from not eating the food I was eating is astounding. Just being able to organize my thoughts and think clearly and feel like I can take on more. I just feel emotionally more stable. I can mentally handle more.

Even conversations with friends and family, and being able to emotionally support and give them advice, I feel like that comes more easily now. I don't even know how to describe it. I can just think clearly, you know? It's not weighing me down.

The confidence I have gained goes across everything we have talked about. It has made me just a happier and better person to everyone. Even talking to people I don't even know, I'm more confident. I feel like I can hold a conversation and feel like I'm equal with them. I feel like I'm more fun to be around because I'm more confident in myself. My energy is completely different. I'm not sitting there worrying about how I feel and feeding everyone my sob story.

Now let's talk about this on a scale of 1–10. On a scale of 1–10, how would you currently rate your life mentally?

I'd say a 9.

Where were you before your transformation on a scale of 1–10?

Ugh a 5?

Looking back at it, it was a hard time. It's almost like it is a hurtful thing to even thing about. It's like I see the pain of where I was.

And when the pain of staying the same outweighs the pain of change is when change happens.

Throughout my transformation, I would go back there when I was down and realize that I was getting better still. It pushed me to keep going.

What a great strategy.

How has your body transformation benefited you financially?

Well, for me, it's all about our family. To me personally, the value I give is doing what I do so that you can run the business and provide for our family. I think when I'm doing a better job and when I'm happier doing what I'm doing, I know I'm helping you more, that's helping our family. To me, that is financial for us and it makes me feel good to know that I'm able to help you out in that way where you don't have to worry about the house or the kids or anything. You can just focus on the business and providing. I feel like I'm aiding you in that so therefore I'm financially providing too in that way. Also, not even just the money aspect, I feel like in helping you, since you're helping so many people, that I'm helping other people.

I found I now have multiple purposes in life and I realize that in helping you, I'm actually helping other people become healthier and live their best life and raising our kids. I'm honored to be doing it.

Now let's talk about this on a scale of 1–10. On a scale of 1–10, how would you currently rate your life financially?

I will say 8 because I think it's great, but, again, you know there's always room for improvement.

Where were you before your transformation on a scale of 1–10?

My mental state of finance and contribution I was giving was probably a 5.

It's not that I didn't think I was contributing before, but mentally I think the way I felt about it was a 5, you know what I mean? I didn't feel confident about it.

How has your body transformation benefited the social relationship area of your life?

I've got to tell you, it's funny that you say that because I've noticed that recently I'm so much more apt to hang out with my friends, talk to them, text them and keep them in the loop, whereas before I was kind of hiding out I think. Not that I didn't want to talk to them, but I was almost in my own shell. I didn't really want to see people. I was just embarrassed. Even though my friends would never say anything or maybe didn't think that. Maybe it was my own issue. I personally was so embarrassed about myself that I didn't want to see my friends. It wasn't fun for me because it's all I could think about. *Are they noticing? Do I look heavier? What are they thinking right now?*

My thinking was distracting and I couldn't just enjoy them. I'm not distracted anymore. I feel good and in check. Because of that, I don't have to think about anything other than having a great time with them. Now I will take initiative and say, "Let's do something," and I'll text my friends. It's become so much more important to me now. Not that it wasn't before, but I'm so much more confident that I'm actually being a good friend.

Now let's talk about this on a scale of 1–10. On a scale of 1–10, how would you currently rate your social life?

I would say a 10. I see my friends a lot and they add a lot to my life. I want to keep it that way. I love them.

Where were you before your transformation on a scale of 1–10?

From my point of view, it was a 7. I still had friends. I just wasn't putting as much of an effort into it, you know?

The heart of my philosophy is that the transformation of the mind and body together leads to accelerated transformation in all other areas of life. Do you agree, and what are your thoughts on that?

Absolutely, and I know I've talked about food a lot. I think every time you asked me a question I talked about food and how it would be clouding me and how I feel cleaner with what I've been eating, but the working out and the marriage with nutrition is so important and amazing. Just the combination of that together, you feel like you're unstoppable and you can do anything. The energy you feel, how clean and light you feel is just empowering.

Did the values and goal-setting exercise help you through your transformation? If so, how?

Yes, because I knew the reason why I was doing what I was doing. For me, family is my number one and every time things would get hard during my transformation, I would always go back to that and think, *This is why you are doing this.* It was so I could be a better mom, a better wife, a better daughter, sister, and that's the most important thing to me in the entire world. Just knowing that this was going to be better for the people I love kept me going.

Even my number two and three values of being healthy for myself and knowing I was going to be better able to fulfill my job and my purpose kept me focused on my why and charging through.

Do you feel that the information it gave you will help you keep your results?

Oh my gosh, absolutely. I think once you get there you can't go back, and if you ever do, you know what it feels like to be transformed and at your highest point. It's addicting. You want to get there again no matter what you have to go through. I always want to be in that spot, so I think just knowing where I've gotten and what I felt like at my peak of feeling so good, fulfilled and at peace with myself, I never want to go back to the way it was.

Jeff

Jeff transformed his body by losing over 50 pounds and over 10% body fat.

Jeff, great to see you today. Man, I'm excited to have you. I wanted to start by saying thank you for your time today. I really appreciate it.

Jeff, what are your three highest values in order?

They are family, career growth and social leisure.

What was your goal when you started your body transformation?

To be able to do more. I was growing and my business was growing really, really fast. I knew that I couldn't keep up at the pace that I was working. I was doing a good 16 to 20 hours a day without being in good shape. In fact, I was far from it. I didn't know how out of shape I was until I got going. But I'm one with an addictive personality so I knew I had to get addicted to the process in order to succeed.

It was all about becoming more efficient with my time. I thought being more efficient with my time was eating once a day and just cranking all day. I would wake up in the morning at seven or eight and I would crank to like probably like 11 o'clock at night, spend a half hour eating, work a little more, go to bed and do it all over again. I realized that this wasn't sustainable. I went from being 170 pounds soaking wet in high school to 10 years later being 260 pounds.

Why did transforming your body become a must for you?

Certainly, at that point, I got out of a very bad relationship. I was engaged, called it off and got back together because I was kind of forced out of the situation. A month and a half later, I went back into that relationship and discovered that it really wasn't right. Then I decided to focus more on work and overall growth. I wasn't teaching anymore at that time so it was all about advancing my business. I knew I wanted to put myself around people who could help me grow instead of help me fail. So when I left that relationship, I moved back in with my parents as I was building a house. I ended up going on a couple vacations with my friends Mike and Dave. We were in Clearwater and went jet skiing. I go to put a life vest on and it barely fits. I was just like "Oh man, how am I going to keep on pushing and growing?" I knew that for everything to grow, I needed to simply be in control of all aspects. On that trip I realized I wasn't, because I wasn't in control of myself. The only control that I had was being able to sell and answer the phone and grow my business. I had no control of my life otherwise.

So let's talk about your transformation and the impact it's had on all areas of your life. What we teach is that the transformation of a fit mind and fit body together leads to accelerated transformation in all other areas of life. Let's break that down.

<u>*How has your body transformation benefited your family relationships?*</u>

I've really taken it back and really appreciated it and made more time for it. Before, family was there and they accepted me. But I think there came a point where they just accepted where I was at and didn't tell me what I wanted to hear. It's like when you date somebody and then after you break up, your mother tells you she hated that girl. As soon as I lost weight, I just became a different person and became more open. Now I'm always like, "Just be honest with me. Don't sugarcoat it. We don't have the time for that and I want to grow. I'm not going to be mad, just tell me as it is." I think the biggest challenge was first being honest with myself. Once that happened, the rest was easy. I was always close with my parents, my brother and my sister. But I think that also helped them realize that, you know, I was serious about growth and that I can't do that if people hold anything back.

Overall, this experience has made us closer. It made me appreciate them more. Actually, that year, for Christmas, I gave them all a trip to Disney to thank them. I realized that without them, I wouldn't be where I am and that family was the closest thing that kept me from, you know, jumping over the ledge so to speak after my really bad relationship.

The crazy thing is that I didn't even realize this was happening until I went through my transformation. I was so programmed to hide everything from my bad relationship and pretend like everything was good. When you pretend you are good where you are not, you pretend everything else is good as well, when it isn't.

Now let's talk about this on a scale of 1–10. On a scale of 1–10, how would you currently rate your family life?

Oh, it's definitely a 10.

Where were you before your transformation on a scale of 1–10?

Honestly, in my head, it probably was still a 10, but now judging it and looking back, it was probably a 5 or 6. Years disconnected but you're still there physically. It was just what I came to accept.

How has your body transformation benefited your work life?

You know what? I don't have to work as long during the days because I'm more efficient with my time. The efficiency with time comes from learning the interval workouts that we do in the studios.

Plus, once you're healthier, things come a lot easier. Your brain is freer and not clogged up with fast food or whatever it is. You're just more efficient so it allowed me to budget my time so I can work 18 hours, but now I'm getting twice to three times the amount of stuff done that I normally would have before.

You don't even realize it's like that at the time because it's just become the lifestyle you knew. When that norm changes, you're just, like, holy cow. After a workout, I now have energy for hours and I just go. It's created more time for me to focus on family and social. And honestly, the social goes back to the growth. At the end of the day, I'm a social guy. My relationships are more important than anything in my life whether it's family, personal or business relationships. This is what leads to growth and that's how I live my life.

Now let's talk about this on a scale of 1–10. On a scale of 1–10, how would you currently rate your work life?

I would say that is 100% a 10 and it's because I can manage it. You know, with three companies, now the question is "How can you manage over 100 employees?" Honestly, it's way easier than having one company because I know and I'm smart about it. Where I was spending, you know, a stupid amount of time on little things, I don't have to do that anymore because I know better. Whether it's delegation or just different strategies that you learn along the way, it really stems from, you know, you. You create the environment that you're in.

This enabled me to have lightning focus.

Where were you before your transformation on a scale of 1–10?

I thought it was a 10 then but it was probably less than a 5.

You know, it's funny, if I were in a position where I was today, I probably would have done at least five to 10 million dollars of sales in one year instead of doing one million dollars in sales for my photo booth business. I was holding myself back from creating a new version of my stuff that I have out now. I would have dominated the market and I would have had to have, like, 15 employees. But looking at it, growing up in a blue-collar family, going from making $35,000 teaching to six-plus figures a year selling photo booths, I was like, "Wow that's awesome!" In some aspects, I was living the dream, but when I look back, I'm like, "Was the goal really the money?" And it wasn't, it was the growth.

Do you feel that the transformation of the body has a lot to do with these changes?

Oh 100%. It gives you everything. It all starts from the body, period.

How has your body transformation benefited the social relationship area of your life?

It's the confidence. I mean before I was wearing stuff like polos or like baggy clothes. We live in a world where you know 71% of people are overweight and I always cared about my image because, especially in my one business, image was everything. I was sales for that business. If I didn't do it, there wouldn't be any. I was great at building those relationships, but I'm sure people would look at me and say, "Man, that guy could lose some weight." What I needed at the time was someone to be honest with me instead of afraid to step on my toes or make me upset. Sure, you may hurt these relationships in the immediacy, but in the long run, they are going to say thank you. My friends weren't at that place where they were able to tell me.

For me, the confidence grew the stronger I got. It was more a mental thing and not as much a physical thing. It was that my body was changing, and I knew I was stronger, but the body didn't matter, it was the mental state that created that. And it's the same right now. I'm in the best shape I've ever been in, but I don't view it that way because I know that there's always something better. I have higher goals for myself now and the goals change. It's not even just losing weight, it's that I've gotten to this level, and why would I stop? What's the point in stopping now? I'm going to get stronger. For me, I don't want to build muscle. I don't need to be shredded for anybody. I just got engaged and I could get the dad bod, but I don't care about that. I care about the speed. I want to be faster. So how do I get faster? By doing different things in the gym and really pushing myself, which I'm working on right now. Being faster in the gym coincides with being faster and more efficient in every aspect of my life.

Now let's talk about this on a scale of 1–10. On a scale of 1–10, how would you currently rate your social life?

Oh, it's definitely a 10.

And you want to know what? There are less people in my life now.

It was that I was trying to please everyone in my big circle. Don't get me wrong, I do care about all of them, but there comes a point where you realize who your true friends are. The ones who were always real with you. These are the ones that you may not always appreciate at the time but they gave you what you needed. My social circle is actually 10 times bigger now, but I also know who my real friends are in that circle. Not just the ones that you want to go and hang out and go grab a beer at the bar with. I'll be the first one to do anything for anybody, but I'm the last one to ask anybody for favors. What's more important to me is being real with me, being straight up, appreciating me for who I am and not taking advantage of me.

I spent most of my 20s in a really good state money-wise and I was taken advantage of. I just didn't realize it. I think that's why most of my friends are a lot older than I am because they're at the same mental state that I am. I was 20 and I was teaching high school. I graduated college in two and a half years, so it was like, who do you hang out with that can understand that? I was in and out of college and didn't have that college experience. I was immediately in a professional, authoritative position. I look back now and think, *Holy shit, I survived that.* Yes, I was learning every year, but looking back, I could have handled it a lot better if I had a better social circle around me to lean on.

Where were you before your transformation on a scale of 1–10?

Realistically, I would probably put it just passing 6.5.

I almost want to put myself as failing because of those few friends that you had that really brought you down. You kept them around because they were fun to be around, but your fun is different when you're mentally clear. I think that's what it really is. I started DJing at 17 years old. I was doing the party thing for like 10 years and that was my life. It came to a point where it was not fun to me. I'd rather be playing the music than sitting around having a drink at a bar. It was just the world I lived and I didn't know any better at the time.

Yeah, I think this goes back to education surprisingly. Because, at the end of the day, my spiritual being is teaching people what I wish I would have known, while being true to myself and never changing who I am. You see people that get into relationships who mold themselves into that person's way of life. For me, being through the really high highs and the really low lows, spirituality is making sure everybody around me, whether it's an employee, a friend or somebody that I just met, understands their self-worth and there's always something to make them grow because there is always good in somebody. That's where my spirituality lies. I want to see people grow because I care about them. If they aren't growing by being around me, then what benefit am I to them?

Let's be honest, you can make a million dollars and be the most miserable person in the world because you're not growing. At the end of the day, everybody wants to grow in some way, shape or form no matter what it is, and what benefit are we to others if we don't help them grow? Imagine if everyone was okay with being okay. People can make a living, they could go get a drink, they could go watch sports and be okay. But what's that saying for us with where we want to be? My goal is that I want everybody to grow. I don't care if it's spiritually, family wise or whatever. If I'm not able to do someone else any good, then why are we even talking? Why are we wasting each other's time if I can't help you grow? I'm here for others.

Now let's talk about this on a scale of 1–10. On a scale of 1–10, how would you currently rate the spiritual area of your life?

I keep on giving myself 10s, but I would say that's a 10. The funny thing is that from when I was teaching, people still come back to me and either apologize for being a jerk to me in school or tell me how I changed their lives. Even yesterday, I was at a party and I ran into a former student who I gave a book. He told me that he still has the book and still makes notes and remembers it. That's what it's about for me.

Where were you before your transformation on a scale of 1– 10?

I'm going to give myself a 9 back when I was still heavy, but I think the level and understanding of what I can do now compared to what I could do is tenfold. I can impact way faster than I ever could. It's not that I wasn't impacting because, let's be honest, there are so many people in this world who don't want to push because they don't want to ruffle feathers. Again, that's just being okay with being okay. I was the one always pushing, but knowing what I know now, I could go back and push those people 10 times as fast.

How has your body transformation benefited you mentally?

I just think the balance in your head is just different. I would wake up in the morning and force myself out of bed because I knew everything I had to do that day. Now I get up and I'm mentally clear and I'm like, "Alright, let's go." Before, I was like, "What good am I going to be able to do for somebody today?" So instead of forcing myself out of bed, I'm ready to go and already thinking about what I'm going to do to help instead of how am I going to get up.

It's the same way when you have a cheat meal. You get up the next morning and you're like, "Oh my God, I shouldn't have eaten that." But you don't get mad about it because that's just life. It's all about how quick you get up and recover moving forward. You still want to live and still have those comfort things, but you question what is really important to you. It's like the bouncy ball effect that you talk about. You may have like two treats a month, but then you may go down to one treat every other month. You do it less because it becomes less important to you. You begin to realize you're more interested in focusing on your purpose.

Now let's talk about this on a scale of 1–10. On a scale of 1–10, how would you currently rate your life mentally?

You know, mentally, I would say with all of the stuff I have going on right now, I'm probably out of a good 9.5 because there is always room for growth. Personally, I don't think anyone could be a 10 in that because you can be as good as you want to be, but there's always room for improvement.

Where were you before your transformation on a scale of 1–10?

Back when I was surviving, I was a good three or four. Honestly, it was from eating that one meal a night and trying to wake up the next morning. That's what I constitute it as because you don't know until you know.

11 o'clock at night eating pizza. Pizza and hot sauce. I'd eat that every night just because it was easy and tasted good. I would like throw it in the oven while I was working. Now, I'm just like, man, I can't even tell you the last time I had a pizza log.

How has your body transformation benefited you financially?

You know financial in money terms does not matter to me at all. At the end of the day, money is money and you can always make more money tomorrow. And I say that being an entrepreneur. For me, financial growth is my time. When it's my time, it's my time. I create that through setting my life up to enable that. Finance is a part of it, but it's only a piece. What's important to me is my dedication to my fiancée, my family and my friends. I do what I do because for me, it's more about experiences than it is money. I'd rather have the experiences than the money. It's always been secondary for me. I could be fine living wherever and having a roof over my head, a nice bed and be happy. The financial aspect of it was always what can I create for myself and others with that?

Throughout my transformation, money became less of a factor for me than it was before. Before it was experiences, and it was also about the money.

I realized after the fact that the experiences mattered more than anything because the experiences are the people; the experiences of going to Egypt and going to Africa, and experiencing life for what it's worth. Now I can come home and be of more value to my group of friends knowing what I have experienced doing these trips. They aren't for me to show off; they are to create a world around me that is not naive to what's going on. The financial part enables it, but I think it goes back to the social part of it for me. It's what can I give to other people so they don't make the same mistakes that I made from the time I was 20 to 29.

Now let's talk about this on a scale of 1–10. On a scale of 1–10, how would you currently rate your life financially?

From an experience standpoint, I enable people to live better now, so you know it's definitely a 10. People see how I live my life. It's very simple. I'm having five shakes a day, so what does it cost me? A banana, kale and some protein powder? When I go away, it's a different story because it's about the experiences. I've made people realize that it's not about what you have here, it's about the experiences you have along the way and what you can share with other people. Before, it was, "Look at my BMW that I bought." I sold it six months later because I realized it wasn't important. I was 27 and apparently I still didn't get it. I just didn't have the vision that I do now.

This has made me very clear on what's important. Your body comes first because you can't worry about anyone else without being in a good state yourself first. It allows me to be more selfless. This is when my close circle became a lot less but my worth became a lot more. Now my circle is back up to being very large, but the people around me are more real because I rebuilt it this way.

Where were you before your transformation on a scale of 1– 10?

I kind of want to give myself a 0 there.

Really?

Yeah, because I didn't know. I mean, why didn't they teach us this in kindergarten? We would all be in such a better place.

How has your body transformation benefited the physical area of your life?

Well, I'm not huffing and puffing all day long. I thought I was in the best physical shape in my life when I turned 31. I was working out like three or four days a week. Now I'm 34 and I'm much more powerful. It's not like I'm showing off, it's more of the fact that I'm in the driver's seat. That drives me in every other aspect of my life. It's become more of a tool for me. I go and work out in the morning. I get to see my friends I've been working out with for years, and also it gives me the energy to move throughout the day and be more efficient because I'm clear. You leave there and you did what you needed to do, you're sweating like crazy but you accomplished it. If you didn't go, what did you accomplish? You skip a day, and you're already off on a bad foot.

It's the best high. I always said when I would DJ and played a number one song and people were screaming was the number one natural high that you can get. Then I started working out.

Now let's talk about this on a scale of 1–10. On a scale of 1–10, how would you currently rate the physical area of your life?

You know, like I said, I'm in the best shape that I've ever been in, but I'm going to put myself at a 9 because I know that I want to grow more. Like I said, the muscle part of it, I just want to be stronger, faster, more agile and more efficient in all areas of life. As most people age, they become less agile. I want to be the opposite.

Where were you before your transformation on a scale of 1–10?

I was on that train that didn't have enough coal and I was just chugging along and it was barely chugging. I was eating the coal and not even moving. I was so sluggish and didn't even know. That was my life for like 13 years. Honestly, I was at a 0.

Wow, how long did it take you to really start feeling a difference?

It took me about three weeks; then it became a lifestyle. That's why, you know, I limit myself with treats because I don't want to break that lifestyle. Again, my biggest strength and my biggest flaw is my want to grow. When you constantly are eating garbage, it becomes your lifestyle real quick. Then where do you go from there? I know that and won't go down that hole again.

The heart of my philosophy is that the transformation of the mind and body together leads to accelerated transformation in all other areas of life. Do you agree, and what are your thoughts on that?

I 100% agree with that. That has always been the mission of this company, it just wasn't said as simply as that. You have to believe in yourself before anyone else can believe in you. If you don't believe in yourself, how can you get other people to buy into what you do? I don't care if you're married for 50 years, if you lose it, you'll lose it and nobody can give it back to you but yourself. So you need to be mentally clear in order to be useful to anyone else, otherwise you're so concentrated on just picking yourself up and surviving.

There comes a point where a light bulb clicks. It doesn't happen overnight, but you get there and you're just like holy shit. At that point, there is no going back. You know too much. That becomes your new high for life.

Did the values and goal-setting exercise help you through your transformation? If so, how?

Yes, they did. With the values and goals, being a teacher you're always asking those types of questions to your students. I always knew them, but I didn't really study it myself because I was too worried about other people. What I realize now is that I should have been doing the same thing for myself. I was in a place where I was really good at helping other people, but I was not good at helping myself. The only way I was able to bring that together was starting at the physical area. Then things just lined up much better.

Do you feel that the information I gave you will help you keep your results?

Yeah, I mean it's in your head now. It's something that you now utilize every day. You can't make that stuff up. It didn't just come out of nowhere. I think, honestly, it's as simple as that.

If you're not mentally clear, then you're not on. I have to be a 100% clear because if I'm not, I'm doing the people I'm working with a disservice. I know what I can offer them when I'm 100%. If I'm 99%, it's like I'm failing them.

Taylor

Taylor transformed her body by losing over 50 pounds.

Taylor, thank you for joining me today to talk about how fit mind plus fit body equals a fit life. I'm pumped to have you here.

Taylor, what are your three highest values in order?

First is being comfortable with myself. Second is my attitude and mindset. Third is just better overall health.

What was your goal when you started your body transformation?

I just wanted to, honestly, lose the 20 pounds, learn how to maintain it by myself and be on my way. I didn't even think I had more than 20 pounds to lose at the time. So, when it kept falling off, it was like an addiction almost. An addiction to feeling good.

I was at a point where I would not leave the house unless I could find an outfit that I felt hid my body from head to toe, and I was just so sick of it. I'd get invited out to things and it was like, "Oh, shit. Now I have to find something that somehow hides me, and people are going to want to take pictures." I was just sick of feeling embarrassed honestly. I wasn't a big mama, I was an average size, but I just could not stand the way I felt in clothes.

Why did transforming your body become a must for you?

I was trying on wedding dresses for the wedding and I was like "Okay, it's time to make a change because what's supposed to be feeling like the most beautiful moment in my life actually feels very dark."

That does it, right?

I kept putting it off. The wedding was in November and I thought eventually time was going to creep up on me and I would just be able to just figure it out on my own. Then, when I jumped into the challenge this June, it was literally the best thing I could have done for myself.

So let's talk about your transformation and the impact it's had on all areas of your life. What we teach is that the transformation of a fit mind and fit body together leads to accelerated transformation in all other areas of life. Let's break that down.

<u>How has your body transformation benefited you spiritually?</u>

Oh my gosh. I don't honestly even know where to start with that question because it took me by total surprise. I started losing weight and I didn't get a different attention necessarily, but with all the positive reinforcement I was getting from my friends and family, I just felt different. During the weight loss, I was going through some family stuff, so my personal life was changing. I was telling my mom the other day that honestly it felt like a rebirth. I don't feel the same at all as I did six months ago.

I have no problem now jumping into conversations and I've made a lot of new friends where I wouldn't have really had the courage to step out of my comfort zone before. I would tell my husband when I would go out with my friends it was a chore because I didn't want to be put in those conversations, to make conversations. It's become a lot better where it doesn't feel like a hassle. I actually get to go out and build new relationships with people. I wasn't able to do that before.

My circle has been super small. Having a larger circle has definitely kept me busy and really makes you feel better about yourself having more people who want to be a part of your life.

Now let's talk about this on a scale of 1–10. On a scale of 1–10, how would you currently rate the spiritual area of your life?

Oh my gosh, 10. It's thriving totally.

I almost felt like at that point I was able to play bigger and ask for things because I deserved it. I finally felt like myself. Things started really exploding for me at that point with the Core Capacity opportunity and many other things.

Where were you before your transformation on a scale of 1–10?

Probably about a 3. This is really a transformation that isn't visible to everybody. It's just how I carry myself and how I live now.

How has your body transformation benefited you mentally?

I just put so many limits on myself that I didn't even realize at the time. Looking back now, I could have taken many things further or stepped outside the box more, but I just didn't have the confidence or the belief in myself to do so.

I was angry and unhappy because I thought where I was in my life was my end-all. I had just graduated college last year, in December, got a full-time job and I was miserable. I hated it. I thought, *I can't believe I rushed through college to do this the rest of my life.* I remember I was praying at my desk completely unplanned, asking for the courage to just walk away and jump into what I really wanted to do. I gave my notice that day. When I started losing weight, I realized, "Wait a second. I don't have to do this or fit into a certain mold." I actually started blogging because I felt like everyone thinks they should be at a certain place at a certain time, which gets us discouraged. My question was who set these standards? That weight just completely got lifted and since then I've felt positive and empowered all of the time.

I will say it a million times. I couldn't believe the difference I have felt on the inside. I just feel like I can seriously do anything I put my mind to. It's actually sad because you don't realize how many limits you put on yourself in so many areas because of the fact that you're uncomfortable, unhappy or just not confident enough.

When I started losing weight and feeling different about myself, I was able to identify who I was on the inside because it was clear. When I was uncomfortable, all I could pay attention to were my physical attributes. I learned that I had so much to offer that was hidden before by 50 freaking pounds.

It's crazy because just six months ago, I was your typical 21-year-old. Now, I feel like I'm a much wiser, mature 22-year-old just because of it. I just didn't think it would have that kind of impact.

Now let's talk about this on a scale of 1–10. On a scale of 1–10, how would you currently rate your life mentally?

I rate it at an 11. This is my biggest strength right now.

Where were you before your transformation on a scale of 1–10?

I was at a struggling 2. Your mind is so powerful. I was trying to grab on to this long before the weight loss and something just wasn't clicking. I think a big part of it is believing what you are thinking and I wasn't believing it.

How has your body transformation benefited the physical area of your life?

Well, I used to be tired all the time. We were actually in and out of the doctors for a while because we thought something was wrong with my thyroid. That totally went away with just a change in diet. So, I have more energy to do more and not waste as much time like I was just hanging out on a couch.

It honestly saves me a lot of money because I stopped going out to eat and going out for drinks so often with my friends. I realized how much I actually did that when I cut that out.

A lot of people think eating healthy is expensive, but you don't realize how much you go out socially and spend in other things that aren't needed. It's really a misperception.

It's tough at first, but you learn and develop a routine quick. Just like anything you start that you don't know yet, it's going to be difficult and time-consuming to learn. It's just a question of "Is this worth it to you or not?"

Now let's talk about this on a scale of 1–10. On a scale of 1–10, how would you currently rate the physical area of your life?

I would say an 8 because I still think I've got some room to improve. I'm learning that I really like to feel strong and I never thought I could lift weights before. Now that's something that is very appealing to me.

Before, when I was trying to lose weight, I would just knock out as much cardio as I could fit into seven days. I wasn't seeing the shrinkage in my waist or the toning up in my arms and my legs because I wasn't doing the right thing. I had the misconception like many others that I was going to bulk up like some bodybuilder chic.

I don't think I'll ever rate physical as a 10 because as soon as I do, I may get complacent and start working out three times per week instead of four or five and just falling off.

Where were you before your transformation on a scale of 1–10?

A big fat 0. I was so off and it was depressing.

Like I said, I wasn't understanding. I was 170 pounds and in the mirror it seemed like the same, but just sitting there I could feel the fat lying over my jeans sometimes and I was like, "Holy crap."

Well, as far as just wealth of knowledge. I feel like I'm rich in guidance as a tool for others who are where I was and that to me is just completely priceless.

What justified the process for me is I was doing personal training before: two sessions a week. I was paying 50 bucks a session for 30 minutes. I was eating a lot of Panera, which is not so great for you, and I wasn't losing any weight. I was like "What the heck?" When I broke it down with Core Capacity, I found that I get five sessions per week at about 20 bucks per session. That's really what sold me and I ran with it. That kept me on track for sure.

Now let's talk about this on a scale of 1–10. On a scale of 1–10, how would you currently rate your life financially?

I would say that's an 8. I'm just jumping into a new field that I don't have an extensive background in yet. I still have a lot to learn and share.

Where were you before your transformation on a scale of 1–10?

I would say a 3. I dipped into other programs here and there and had some success but nothing measurable to this.

How has your body transformation benefited your family relationships?

My relationships with my family got so much better and that was really unexpected.

My mom used to ask me, "What's wrong? What's wrong?" and I used to get so upset because I felt like nothing was wrong. I didn't know what she was getting or picking up, but she would be like, "I know my daughter. Something is wrong." Honestly, nothing was ever genuinely wrong. I just must have carried this dark, bummed-out persona all the time and didn't even realize it.

She would even say, "It's hard to be around you sometimes because it just feels like you have this rain cloud over you and it's like you're not acknowledging that there's something," and that would upset me even more.

That was a hard wake-up call for sure. I'm glad that I didn't learn that until it was better already.

Now let's talk about this on a scale of 1–10. On a scale of 1–10, how would you currently rate your family life?

It's a 10 for sure.

Where were you before your transformation on a scale of 1–10?

It was at a solid 6. I've always had great relationships, but now they call me the bright light of the family. They say I always have so much energy and uplifting positive things to add, even when they may be talking about a not-so-great situation. I'm the person who now turns it around and switches it to the light side. I'm so blessed to be that person in people's lives now.

You said your family calls you the light now. What would they have called you before?

I would say trying. I was always trying to better myself with something, but I was always falling short in one aspect or another. Now I feel like I can do anything. It's very symbolic for me because I feel like this is where my new life is headed. I'm a drastically different woman than I was six months ago. I didn't think I could change so much in such a little time.

Sometimes when I hear myself talk about myself I think, *Am I being boastful? Am I conceited, or am I just really comfortable, and confident and happy with who I am?* I've just never felt that before. It's indescribable.

My integrity grew too. Even something as small as being in a grocery store when you pick something up, and then you just want to set it down or whatever. I started to take integrity in those small moments where no one was looking because now I'm confident in front of people, but what am I doing behind closed doors? Now I take it back. This is just an example, but I really feel like my character all along has transformed.

How has your body transformation benefited your work life?

Well, it has transformed it from 0 to a 100. I felt like I completely hit a brick wall when I was in that job I was telling you about. I had also just graduated college and was 30 grand in debt thinking to myself, *I'm making less here than I am with my waitress job, and I hate it on top of it.* I was also in grad school pursuing my master's degree in Criminal Justice, which I knew I wasn't going to do. I finally made the decision to just stop investing time and money in something that I already knew wasn't for me. I felt like a failure at that point because it was just months away from my wedding, and my fiancé and I were still living with our parents because I was not making enough money. I found myself just serving at Duffs and I was like "Wow, this is not where I want to be." I felt like I lost hope and that's why I let myself do the challenge. I knew I needed to give myself a purpose.

Honestly, I don't think it was a coincidence whatsoever that I quit my job and came into Core Capacity. I think that was really purposeful, I think God knew this was going to happen a long time before I did.

If only you would have known me a couple of years ago. I had two years left of college and I would be crying about the possibility of not having a job after college. I just felt like I had to be in control of every single step of my life. Letting go was just never an option for me. I actually ended up in the hospital in 2015 because I just had crippling anxiety over my future. I was like, "Okay, if this is what I get for trying to control all aspects of my life, that obviously is not working out very well." I just needed to go with the flow and let things fall into place, and that's exactly what happened the minute I stopped doing that.

Now let's talk about this on a scale of 1–10. On a scale of 1– 10, how would you currently rate your work life?

Well, I'd say it's a 10. As these next couple months go by, I'm going to be dipping my toes into a new business venture I never thought I would be getting into. I'm super excited and I'm ready.

Where were you before your transformation on a scale of 1– 10?

I would say probably a 1. I was feeling very unsuccessful. I literally have jumped the scale in every aspect and I know that very well. It's empowering all the way around.

How has your body transformation benefited the social relationship area of your life?

Honestly, a lot of my new friends in my circle I've met through Core Capacity. I told my mom, "This company is a breeding ground for people like me." I didn't think there were so many people with similar values like me until I was exposed to it here.

I just felt like I fit in finally. In high school, I was not that girl, and then in college, I just couldn't be that girl because I was in a serious relationship the whole time. I've never had that circle of friends and it's just so refreshing to have that now. Looking back, it was so silly because I held myself back from so many things.

Now let's talk about this on a scale of 1–10. On a scale of 1– 10, how would you currently rate your social life?

Oh, definitely a 10. I am just transformed all around. I can talk to anybody and I want to talk to people and build relationships with them.

Where were you before your transformation on a scale of 1–10?

Socially, I'd say I was a 4. I was trying to put myself in situations where I was comfortable, but I would never step outside that zone.

The heart of my philosophy is that the transformation of the mind and body together leads to accelerated transformation in all other areas of life. Do you agree, and what are your thoughts on that?

I would have never believed that if I didn't experience it for myself.

It's really a sad, hidden concept that gets brushed under the rug that you can change all aspects of your life by changing yourself physically. It almost sounds artificial, because you think, *Well, it doesn't matter what it looks like,* but it matters how you feel about yourself. Changing my body gave that to me. I think that's what it really comes down to because that is the person we put out to others. I'm the light of my family where before I was trying.

Like I said, it's something that is almost blinding until you can shed a few of those pounds so you can start getting a little taste of what it's like to feel content. I'm so fortunate to have been exposed to it and I honestly thank you a lot for it. Because I was very afraid to believe and when I did, I realized how solid this system actually was.

Did the values and goal-setting exercise help you through your transformation? If so, how?

Well, at first, I was one of those narrow-minded people that were just saying, "Let me lose the 20 pounds and I'll be on my way." I didn't really understand at the time. Now I think it was very beneficial because as I sat there doing it, I realized I didn't have these things premeditated. I had to really think about how it was affecting the other areas of my life. From that day forward was when my eyes started to really open to that concept.

Do you feel that the information I gave you will help you keep your results?

Yeah, I do. I think it's ongoing accountability that is tangible. The people we care about most are the ones we influence and who also influence us. It's about being the best you can be at all times for the people so you can always put your best foot forward.

Andrea

Andrea transformed her body by losing over 100 pounds.

Andrea, I'm really excited to talk to you today and thank you very much for joining me today.

Andrea, what are your three highest values in order?

Mental, social and spiritual.

What was your goal when you started your body transformation?

Really to lose weight. I don't really remember having a number in mind. I knew I wanted to lose a substantial amount of weight but I never said I wanted to lose 100 pounds in a year. I just wanted to, number one, feel better about myself and get healthier because I knew health-wise I wasn't in good shape. I was tipping the scale at 300 pounds. Being only 5'4" obviously that was not a good thing. I hadn't been to the doctor in a couple years just because I was scared to. I was afraid of what they were going to say. I just I knew I wasn't healthy. The number really wasn't that important to me at that point of my transformation.

I've been overweight my entire life. Being almost 300 pounds is the heaviest I've ever been, but I've always been heavy. I've tried Weight Watchers, ADVO care, beach body, literally everything out there. Seeing how successful other people were with what you do, I knew I had nothing to lose at that point but weight really.

Why did transforming your body become a must for you?

I walked into the Tonawanda studio where I was going to sign up for my first challenge. That's where I met Tom. I went to turn my application in and freaked out a little bit. I sat down with Tom and just right there in the open and started throwing out excuses to him and he just wasn't accepting them from me. He had a solution for everything that I was giving him. I truly believed that he knew how much I needed him and that place. He wasn't going to let me walk out of that door without starting it. Tom knew how much I needed that place. It was right there in that moment that my life changed. The decision became finalized for me.

So let's talk about your transformation and the impact it's had on all areas of your life. What we teach is that the transformation of a fit mind and fit body together leads to accelerated transformation in all other areas of life. Let's break that down.

How has your body transformation benefited you mentally?

In every way possible. That's why it's my number one. I'm just in a better state of mind. My confidence has changed drastically. Now I wake up every day, you know, excited to tackle the day. I never used do that. I used to, you know, dread going to work and just going through like the movements in life. My outlook on life is just so much more positive. I embrace every day now as more of an opportunity to better myself and the people that I love. My confidence has definitely been the number one thing for sure. Not even just like the way that I look, it's how I feel like inside too.

I was distracted before too. I love helping other people and that wasn't happening. Something I hear all the time now from people in the gym is how inspirational and motivational I am now. Besides changing my own life, the most rewarding thing about all of this is being able to help other people. People come up to me all the time and say, "I saw your video," or, "I saw you working out and you have helped me so much." I can't tell you how many people have messaged me on Facebook and have asked me questions. That has seriously been the best thing ever. Through helping myself, now I just want to help other people that are in the same exact spot that I was a year and a half ago. This is not about me anymore because I've already been helped. I just want to help other people because it's not easy. If it were, everyone would be doing it.

Now let's talk about this on a scale of 1–10. On a scale of 1–10, how would you currently rate your life mentally?

I'm not perfect but definitely a 9. I think there is always room for improvement. No one is perfect and honestly that's not sustainable and not needed.

When you're in it, you don't really think it's that bad. Then you come out on the other side and realize, "Wow, that was bad." You just don't see it before that moment.

Where were you before your transformation on a scale of 1–10?

Probably like a 3 or 4. Yeah, not good at all.

How has your body transformation benefited the social relationship area of your life?

Again with the confidence. When I'm out, I have so much confidence talking to people and I'm not self-conscious in the way that people may be judging what I'm wearing or what I look like. It's really helped my overall energy, enthusiasm and really in every way possible. When I went out before, I was surviving. Now I'm thriving.

Like I said, I was always overweight. When I was in grad school, I had really started packing on the pounds as I got closer and closer to 30. When I was younger, I was always very photogenic and loved being in front of the camera. I got to the point where I didn't want to have any pictures taken of me anymore. That's when I knew, *Okay, something is actually wrong,* because that was not me. I started hiding and that was another trigger that this was going in the wrong direction.

Now I'm not hiding at all. I'm definitely not a center of attention type of person, but I am by no means hiding. I would say I'm more of a thriving, confident person now.

Now let's talk about this on a scale of 1–10. On a scale of 1–10, how would you currently rate your social life?

Oh, it's a 10 for sure.

Where were you before your transformation on a scale of 1–10?

I would probably say about a 4-5.

How has your body transformation benefited you spiritually?

I'm not the most religious person, but I do believe that that my relationship with God has improved. But also I feel like I've found my purpose. I feel like this is what I was meant to do and I tell people that all the time. I've found a true love for it. My background is in sports medicine and physical therapy. I had, you know, education in this area and I'm just now going through all of this, I just feel like it's all connected and come full circle. I feel like this has been like the missing piece for me. I just kind of feel more complete. I feel my purpose is now fulfilled and it's all about helping other people feel better about themselves.

You're just so much more thankful now, you're encouraged, thankful, encouraged, motivated with everything. I think you really need to be in a bad place to really understand what good feels like. I'm a firm believer in that.

Now let's talk about this on a scale of 1–10. On a scale of 1–10, how would you currently rate the spiritual area of your life?

I would say it's a 9.

Where were you before your transformation on a scale of 1–10?

Probably about a 3.

Like I said, the purpose for me is just huge, you know? Spreading the good word, encouraging others and just spreading overall positivity and good vibes is my focus. I'm just shouting from the rooftop about all of this because it's just so important. It's definitely been the final piece of the puzzle for me.

How has your body transformation benefited you financially?

I think when people think about finance and losing weight they think, *Oh my goodness losing weight is too expensive* or, *Eating healthy is too expensive. I can't afford that.* I think that's the first thing people think of. I used to be one of those people for sure. Going through the program, I quickly learned that that's not really the case. It's just simple eating and it's really not expensive compared to everything you were eating before. That's been a huge awakening for me.

With my work, I'm now able to be on my feet throughout the workday. I don't get tired like I did when I was heavier. As far as my self-worth, it goes back to being able to help other people. To be able to be that ear to listen or to share knowledge of an experience with people has been invaluable to me.

Like I said before, I can't tell you how many people have come up to me or messaged me and asked me for help or tips and tricks. It's amazing. It's worth so much to me to just be able to help somebody. I don't think you can put a dollar amount on it. It gives me a feeling of fulfillment in my life to be able to help somebody else. You just can't put a number on it.

I truly don't know where I would be without this place, I really don't.

Working in health care, I work with patients every single day and I see how unhealthy people are. It's crazy how many medications they take daily. It's really sad to see. In the long run, you are really saving yourself money by investing in yourself now. Prescriptions, medications, hospital visits, doctor's visits, and surgeries. Investing in yourself now is truly not only going to save your life but save you so much money down the road. Not to mention, the quality you will be able to experience during that time is immeasurable.

Now let's talk about this on a scale of 1–10. On a scale of 1– 10, how would you currently rate your life financially?

I would probably say about an 8.

Where were you before your transformation on a scale of 1– 10?

Probably about a 4.

How has your body transformation benefited your family relationships?

My family doesn't live here. My family lives in New Jersey. I've always considered my friends like my family just because I've lived away from home for so long. They've really been my rock throughout all this. That sense of community and just knowing that you're not alone. Someone is always going to have your back.

It's interesting because you think your same friends will always be there in your life, but I've also experienced people who have not been the most encouraging. Saying negative comments of, "Oh, you are going to gain the weight back," or, "I can't believe you are spending all that money, that's stupid." In the beginning, it's very discouraging and you are scared, you know? That said, I'm the type of person who wants to prove others wrong and show you that I can do it. Really, the haters were pushing me even harder to get what I wanted. They pushed me the entire way and, honestly, I think they helped me the most through this. It's been very eye opening.

The relationships with my friends have definitely improved for the better. We are able to do so much more together now. I will say though that the other relationships I have created throughout my journey have really been the most rewarding part of this for me. My friends who have been with me throughout this entire transformation have obviously been amazing and will always be number one to me, but the family that I have gained through my transformation has also been extremely powerful and wonderful.

Just having a common ground in your circle of people who share the same values, goals and motivation that you do is so rewarding. You know you always have someone in your corner supporting you whether you're having a bad day or you're having a really good day. It's incredible.

Now let's talk about this on a scale of 1–10. On a scale of 1–10, how would you currently rate your family life?

I would say a 10.

Where were you before your transformation on a scale of 1–10?

I would say it was a 6.

How has your body transformation benefited your work life?

I'm able to perform my job better. I'm on my feet all day no problem now. I feel so much more confident dealing with medical professionals. It's almost like you feel like they take you more seriously. You never feel confident being the overweight person in the medical field. You feel like people are looking at you saying, "Well, she's not taking her own advice." You would feel like they were judging you. I feel like people just look at me in a much more positive way than they did before for sure.

That has boosted my confidence and just my overall happiness so much. People tell me often, "You're always just so happy." Well, I do know that, in reality, I do exhibit all things. I'm not completely a bubbly, happy person all the time. What I would say is that I'm overall a happy person because I have a lot to be happy about and I have a lot to be thankful for.

Before, I was stressful, emotional, and not confident to talk to professionals or management. I was always hiding. Now my whole demeanor and energy have become so much more positive.

Now let's talk about this on a scale of 1–10. On a scale of 1–10, how would you currently rate your work life?

It's a 9.

Where were you before your transformation on a scale of 1–10?

It was probably at a 3.

How has your body transformation benefited the physical area of your life?

Physically, I'm just able to do much more. I'm stronger than I have ever been in my entire life, both mentally and physically. I've always been an athlete, but I can truly say that, at almost 31, I am the strongest I've ever been.

Even just the little things like going up the stairs. I don't care if it was five steps or 30. When I was heavier, I was always out of breath going up the stairs. Now I can go up the stairs at the mall and not be out of breath at all. Before, there was no way. I was sweating and out of breath.

I'm also presenting myself much differently with my appearance because of my confidence. Before, I was wearing a lot of sweatpants and sweatshirts to cover up. I still like my loungewear, but it's just different now because it's not all the time.

Although changing my entire wardrobe out has been a bit pricey, I love wearing my clothes now because I feel great in them. It's absolutely worth it.

Health used to also be a big concern for me as well. A few years ago, I was hospitalized for five days and before I was admitted to the hospital, I had to get pre-screening like blood work done. My doctor told me that my A1C was elevated. I knew that was not a good thing. If I would have needed surgery, the doctor told me I was not a candidate to have it done laparoscopically because of my size. I was too big. I ended up not needing the surgery, but just hearing that I wasn't a candidate because of my size was a kick to the gut. I thought, *If I was smaller, this wouldn't be an issue.* I knew something needed to change. I was on the brink of turning 30 and I really wanted to lose the weight before I turned 30. I'm so glad I did.

Now let's talk about this on a scale of 1–10. On a scale of 1–10, how would you currently rate the physical area of your life?

Physically, I'd say 9. I want to say a 10, but I don't want to do that. I feel there is always room for improvement and I'm definitely not perfect.

As much as I love my body now, I don't beat myself up about it if I fall off for a second. I don't ever expect to be perfect, have the perfect body or be the perfect weight. The biggest thing to me is the fact that where I am now is leaps and bounds ahead from where I was.

Where were you before your transformation on a scale of 1–10?

I think that was at a 2.

The heart of my philosophy is that the transformation of the mind and body together leads to accelerated transformation in all other areas of life. Do you agree, and what are your thoughts on that?

Oh, 110%. You know, I guess I didn't realize going into this how true that is. I had heard you talk about all of this before, but having gone through it, you really see how everything comes together and how everything is affected. I think most people just go into it just thinking it's a number, and that they just want to lose weight. As you go through it, the farther you progress, you see how everything else in your life is affected. Everything is just turned to a positive direction. It's crazy to see how everything kind of comes together and that puzzle fits together perfectly. I call it a puzzle just because you need all of those pieces and areas of life for it to work.

Did the values and goal-setting exercise help you through your transformation? If so, how?

Oh, for sure. It helped me keep my mind right and reminded me why I started in the first place. It kept my positivity going because you're not always going to have good days. In the beginning, you are going to have tough days. It's important to be reminded a lot and this gives it to you. Finding your why and staying connected to the reason you even started your journey in the first place. I think it's very easy to lose if you don't stay connected. Reflecting back on that just keeps you focused.

Do you feel that the information I gave you will help you keep your results?

Oh, for sure, 100%. Yes, absolutely.

Something as simple as writing this down and having it as a tool is awesome. I also think as we progress and move through our goals, what's most important to us changes. Keeping up on this keeps you current with what is really going on inside.

CLOSING THOUGHTS

Interestingly, but also what seems obvious from the outside, is that as people gained a better understanding of their highest values and transformed their health, their perception of themselves and the love they had for themselves grew. This blossomed into confidence and the rest of the transformation took care of itself in all areas of life because of that one simple thing everyone here experienced. They became happier with themselves. They began to love themselves more, which led to confidence and transformation spreading into all other areas of life.

REFERENCES

1. Demartini, John. "The Breakthrough Experience." *The Breakthrough Experience*, 14-15 Apr. 2012, Marriot Hotel, Houston TX. 11-12 Jan. 2013, Marriot Hotel, Houston TX. 7-8 Oct. 2017, Hyatt Regency Hotel, Toronto CA.

2. Danes, Chuck, "The Law of Polarity." *www.abundance-and-happiness.com,* 2005, www.abundance-and-happiness.com/law-of-polarity.html, Accessed 2005.

3. Hill, Napoleon, Epilogue Berges, Steve. *Think And Grow Rich: Collector's Edition.* American Liberty Press, Jan 2010, pp. 118

4. Lipton, Bruce. *The Wisdom Of The Cells: How Your Beliefs Control Your Biology.* Sounds True, Incorporated, 1 Sep. 2006. Audiobook. Chapter 6, 27:11, Chapter 1, 1:01:51.

5. Rohn, Jim. *"Treat your body like a temple."* The *Inspiring Journal,* www.theinspiringjournal.com, 13 May 2017, www.theinspiringjournal.com/treat-your-body-likea-temple-not-a-woodshed, 13 May 2017.

6. Jung, C.G. *Synchronicity: An Acausal Connecting Principle.* Princeton, New Jersey: Princeton University Press. 1969, pp.109–110

7. McCarty, Rollin. *Science of the Heart Volume 2.* HeartMath Institute, 2015.

8. Sherer, Steve. *"Your Heart Controls Your Brain."* Dexter Patch, www.patch.com, 24 May 2013. https://patch.com/michigan/dexter/bp--your-heartcontrols-your-brain. 24 May 2013.

9. Hill, Napoleon. *Think And Grow Rich.* The Ralston Society, 1937.

10. Demartini, J.F. *The Breakthrough Experience*. Hay House, Inc. 2002, pp. 12.

11. Gerber, Michael. *The E-Myth Revisited*. Harper Audio, 31 May 2005. Audiobook.

12. Emerson, R.W. *"Self-Reliance."* Archived VCU Websites, 1841. American Transcendentalism Web, https://archive.vcu.edu/english/engweb/transcendentalism/authors/emerson/essays/selfreliance.html

13. Demartini, John. "Demartini Method Training Program." The Demartini Method Training Program Live, 23-27 Oct. 2012, Marriot Hotel, Houston TX. 16-20 Oct. 2013, Marriot Hotel, Houston TX. 3-7 Sep. 2015, Marriot Hotel, Houston TX.

14. Robbins, Mel. *The 5 Second Rule*. Mel Robbins Productions Inc, 22 Feb. 2017.

15. Arrhenius, Svante. *"The Arrhenius Law: Activation Energies."* Chemistry LibreTexts, 30 Oct. 2016, https://chem.libretexts.org/Core/Physical_and_Theoretical_Chemistry/Kinetics/Modeling_Reaction_Kinetics/Temperature_Dependence_of_Reaction_Rates/The_Arrhenius_Law/The_Arrhenius_Law%3A_Activation_Energies, 30 Oct. 2016

16. Lucas, Jim. *"Newton's Laws of Motion." Live Science, 26 Sep. 2017,* https://www.livescience.com/46558-lawsof-motion.html, 26 Sep. 2017.

17. Massimi, Michela. *Pauli's Exclusion Principle.* Cambridge University Press, 2005.

18. Demartini, John. *"Prophecy 1 Experience."* The Prophecy 1 Experience Live, 9-15 Apr. 2013, Marriot Hotel, Houston TX.

19. Rohn, Jim. *The Power of Ambition.* Nightingale Conant, 14 Oct. 2014. Audiobook. Chapter 7, 13:27.

20. Rohn, Jim. *Cultivating an Unshakable Character.* Nightingale Conant, 14 Oct. 2014. Audiobook. Chapter 10, 26:52.

21. Benes, Sarah, Alperin, Holly. *The Essentials of Teaching Health Education.* Human Kinetics, 18 Feb 2016.

22. Maslow, A.H. *"A Theory of Human Motivation."* Psychological Review, 50(4), 1943, pp. 370-396.

23. Robbins, Tony. "The 6 Human Needs." Unleash The Power Within, Meadowlands Expo Center, 5 Mar. 2015, New York. Pp. 9-14.

24. Doran, G.T. *"There's a S.M.A.R.T. way to write management's goals and objectives."* Management Review. AMA FORUM. 70(11), Nov. 1981, pp. 35-36

25. Wade, Nicholas. *"Your Body Is Younger Than You Think."* The New York Times, 2 Aug. 2005, http://www.nytimes.com/2005/08/02/science/your-bodyis-younger-than-you-think.html?_r=0. 2 Aug. 2005.

26. Price, Weston. *Nutrition and Physical Degeneration.* 6th ed. The Price-Pottenger Nutrition Foundation, Inc. 2000.

27. *Cowspiracy: The Sustainability Secret.* Created by Kip Anderson and Keegan Kuhn, contributions by Dr. Richard Oppenlander, Michael Pollan, Dr. Will Tuttle, Howard Lyman, Will Potter, Will Anderson, appearances by Michael Besancon, Michael Klaper, MD, David Robinson Simon, Dr. Kirk R. Smith, Self-Published, 2014.

28. Graham, Douglas N. *The 80/10/10 Diet.* FoodnSport Press, 2006. Pp. 16-18, pp. 23, pp. 99-109, pp. 113, pp. 121.

29. Campbell, Colin T. *"Nutrition Fundamentals."* Plant-Based Nutrition Certificate Program, eCornell College, Nov 2015. Course transcripts, ppts, audio/visual presentations. Ppt. 22, 25, 26, module 2, pp. 16.

30. Campbell, Colin T. *"Diseases of Affluence."* Plant-Based Nutrition Certificate Program, eCornell College, Nov 2015. Course transcripts, ppts, audio/visual presentations.
Ppt. 31.

31. Campbell, Colin T. *"Principals in Practice."* Plant-Based Nutrition Certificate Program, eCornell College, Nov 2015. Course transcripts, ppts, audio/visual presentations.

32. Greger, Michael. *"Paleopoo: What We Can Learn from Fossilized Feces."* www.nutritionfacts.org, volume 29, 17 Feb. 2016. https://nutritionfacts.org/video/paleopoowhat-we-can-learn-from-fossilized-feces/, 17 Feb. 2016.

33. Greger, Michael. *"How much pus is there in milk?"* www.nutritionfacts.org, 8 Sep. 2011, https://nutritionfacts.org/2011/09/08/how-much-pus-isthere-in-milk/, 8 Sep. 2011.

34. Fuhrman, Joel. *Eat To Live,* Little, Brown and Company, 2011, pp. 128-131, pp. 223, pp. 226.

35. Carnegie, Dale, Narrated: MacMillan, Andrew. *How to Win Friends and Influence People.* Simon & Schuster Audio, 17 Sep. 2004, Audiobook, Chapter 2. 16:17.

ACKNOWLEDGEMENTS

First I want to give gratitude and recognition to every challenge we face that we choose to turn into an opportunity.

A very special thank you and acknowledgment goes to:

My brothers Nathan and Tyler for always being there for me and for being my best friends.

My entire team at Core Capacity Transformations for their love, support, inspiration, and the challenge you give to me.

The amazing clients I have the privilege to serve every day with Core Capacity Transformations.

My brothers from another mother: Dr. Steve Novelli, Jeremy Zolnowski and Jeremy Childs.

The incredible mentors I have been so blessed to learn from so far in my life:
- Dad
- Mom
- Laura Buccieri
- My incredible mother and father-in-law
- Dr. John Demartini
- Anthony Robbins
- Grant Cardone
- Russell Brunson
- Sam Bakhtiar
- Pat Rigsby
- The amazing mentors I get to enjoy every day through my

studies.

My dog Wally who is always by my side giving me inspiration and helping me create.

Sunrise Shores for delivering constant inspiration.

831 Design, my publishing company, for their fantastic work.

Every person dedicated to personal growth and maximizing their potential.

Finally, I'd love to thank EVERYONE who has given me positivity or who has added challenge to my life. Without you, growth would be impossible.

BIO - ABOUT THE AUTHOR

"I have been blessed to live a life full of support, love and, thankfully, many challenges. These same challenges have been the greatest enabler's in my life." These are the words of Trevor Buccieri, A mind, body and life transformation strategist on a mission to empower others to become unstoppable in life.

Trevor grew up as an overweight kid after a series of kidney problems left him very inactive. Empowerment and inspiration was the last thing on his mind. What was on his mind was the sob story filled with excuses he constantly ran for himself until the day he "finally woke up."

Trevor says he is so grateful for this time because he now understands exactly why he felt the way he did. He said, "I didn't have a fit mind, I didn't have a fit body, and it was affecting all other areas of my life. How I perceived myself and the actions I was not taking were leading to an ultimate outcome I knew I didn't want and I knew I was better than."

As he began building his first business, Core Capacity Transformations, now a national franchise, he was in a constant battle with a lack of belief in himself. He didn't think he was capable, nor did Trevor think he deserved it. The truth, he realized, is that he "wasn't thinking clearly."

What became very clear to him was his desire to gain understanding, change and ultimately a sense of control with his mind and body. He realized to go any further, changing his perception of himself, giving deeper meaning to his goals and nurturing his body to the best of his ability was a must for growth in all areas of his life.

For nearly 10 years now at the time of this writing, learning, preparing, applying, absorbing and teaching others on a constant cycle of rinse and repeat has become his ever-growing obsession.

Trevor practices an intense daily education regime, which continues to grow as he studies under his great mentors like human behavior and personal development specialist Dr. John Demartini, world authority on leadership psychology, life and business Tony Robbins, neuroscientist Dr Joe Dispenza, Grant Cardone, Russell Brunson, John Maxwell, Jack Canfield, and the list continues with hundreds of other mentors he says he has "been blessed to learn from," and thousands more he says he will keep learning from in the books he reads, seminars he continues to attend, and mentors he coaches with.

Along with his role as CEO and president of Core Capacity Transformations, Trevor is always expanding his outreach on a mission to help others transform their lives, their businesses, and their legacy.

You can find Trevor at www.findyourcapacity.com, and Trevor Buccieri on LinkedIn, Facebook and Instagram.

57722552R00181

Made in the USA
Middletown, DE
02 August 2019